Radical
Political
Economy

Radical
Political
Economy

A Concise Introduction

Charles A. Barone

M.E.Sharpe
Armonk, New York
London, England

Library of Congress Cataloging-in-Publication Data

Barone, Charles A.
 Radical political economy : a concise introduction / Charles A. Barone
  p. cm.
 Includes bibliographical references and index.
 ISBN 0-7656-1364-6 (hc : alk. paper) ISBN 0-7656-1365-4 (pbk. : alk. paper)
  1. Radical economics. I. Title.

HB97.7.B373 2004
335—dc22   2003061605

CONTENTS

LIST OF TABLES AND FIGURES

Tables

Figures

PREFACE

This book grew out of the need for an abbreviated text on radical political economy. The Department of Economics at Dickinson College had created a new undergraduate course on heterodox economics. This course, required of all economics majors, serves as an introduction to several different heterodox economic perspectives. There were few current textbooks or readers on radical economics, fewer still at the introductory level, and none that could be covered adequately in the few weeks of the semester that were allotted to this perspective. The otherwise excellent introductory text, *Understanding Capitalism*, was on the one hand too long and detailed and on the other hand not inclusive enough (Bowles and Edwards 1993).

Radical Political Economy was written to fill the gap in the radical literature. It draws heavily on Bowles and Edwards, especially in chapters 2 and 3, but is much more inclusive and representative of the other strands of radical thought. Although more inclusive of U.S. radical thought, this text is much more concise, and while disagreements are sometimes noted, the many (healthy) debates among radicals are left for the more advanced student. An extensive bibliography of further readings is provided for that purpose at the end of each chapter.

Radical political economy is the intellectual offspring of Marxist economic thought and so we begin with a chapter on Marx's political economy. Chapter 2 focuses on the contemporary radical political economy method, core concepts (surplus, class, and exploitation), and system-defining features of the capitalist economic system. This is followed by a discussion of the radical theory of production and the labor process in chapter 3 that examines profits, capital accumulation, competition, and the contested terrain between workers and capitalists in the workplace.

Chapter 4 extends the basic economic analysis of the previous chapter to the radical analysis of the noneconomic spheres (superstructure) of culture and state. Here the roles of ideology and reproduction are discussed, with emphasis on the roles that education and the media play in capitalism. The nature of the interrelationships of patriarchy and capitalism, along with the role of the state in capitalism, are also covered in chapter 4.

The macrodynamics (laws of motion) of capitalism are examined in chapter 5. Three contradictions of capitalism are emphasized in this chapter: unequal distribution of income and wealth, imperialism, and economic crises.

Finally, chapter 6 critically evaluates capitalist performance in the United States against the criteria of efficiency, quality of life, equity, and democracy, and then presents the radical democratic socialist alternative to capitalism. Past attempts to build socialism and existing forms in other countries are also critically evaluated. Given the poor prognosis for democratic socialism at present, chapter 6 ends with a discussion of some radical proposals for reforming capitalism that, while falling short of democratic socialism, would create a much more egalitarian society.

I want to thank Dickinson College for supporting the inclusion of heterodox economics into the standard economics curriculum; it is one of only a small number of colleges and universities with the intellectual integrity to do so. This text is the outgrowth of those efforts, and I am grateful to have had the opportunity to teach this material to Dickinson students over the past several years. Their engagement of radical political economy has strengthened this text. I also want to thank my economics colleagues for their help in preparing the manuscript for this book, especially Gordon Bergsten who read each draft and made many useful comments that improved the manuscript. Appreciations also go to the publisher, M.E. Sharpe, who since 1958 has played an important role in keeping radical economics and other heterodox intellectual traditions vibrant and growing with its long list of published books and journals.

Radical
Political
Economy

1 HISTORICAL ORIGINS OF RADICAL POLITICAL ECONOMY

The radical intellectual tradition started by Karl Marx never took hold in economics in the United States until the 1960s, when students and a few faculty driven by their concerns about poverty, discrimination, and imperialism began questioning the value of neoclassical economics. They turned to the work of Marxists and other unorthodox thought for guidance. The work of three American Marxists—Paul Baran (1957), Paul Sweezy (1942), and Harry Magdoff (1968)—as well as the German-born but American-educated Andre Gunder Frank (1967) and the Belgian Marxist Ernest Mandel (1962) played an important early role in the formation of ideas that came to be known as radical political economy. (Their most influential works are cited in the references at the end of this chapter.)

Shunned by the mainstream, radical economists in 1968 formed their own professional organization, the Union for Radical Political Economics, and their own professional academic journal, *The Review of Radical Political Economy.* Several other new journals have subsequently been established both in the United States and elsewhere devoted to the publication of radical thought. (These journals are listed under "further reading" at the end of this chapter.) By the mid-1970s a substantial radical economics literature had been written. Radical economics had a large following in the

United States as well as in other countries and had established itself as a viable contender within the discipline. Although still a distinct minority, radical economics has continued to grow, and by the year 2000 radical economists had established themselves at a number of universities and colleges. Graduate programs in radical political economy in the United States are offered at The American University, University of Massachusetts-Amherst, University of California-Riverside, University of Utah-Salt Lake, Notre Dame University, University of New Hampshire, and The New School for Social Research.

Although today radical political economy embraces several different strands of thought, a common research program that emphasizes the importance of class domination, exploitation, inequality, and cyclical instability unites radical economists. Critical of capitalism, radicals look to democratic socialist visions as the basis for solutions to such problems as cyclical instability, unemployment, low wages, poverty, oppressive conditions of work, imperial domination of Third World peoples, and gender and racial inequality.

While some strands of this perspective are faithful to Marx's original ideas, other strands extend and modify Marx's ideas, some quite significantly. Other strands have drawn additionally on the ideas of Thorstein Veblen (and other institutionalists), John Maynard Keynes, Joseph Schumpeter, and Piera Sraffa (and other post-Keynesians). In this introduction, no attempt will be made to capture completely all aspects of this rich intellectual heritage. Rather the focus will be on Marx. Evidence of Marx's philosophical and methodological approach, theory, and concerns can be found to a varying extent in the work of virtually all radical political economists.

Marx's Dialectical Perspective

Marx's approach to understanding the social world has been called "dialectical," a perspective that is quite different from other philosophical stances.[1] A dialectical perspective focuses on the nature of reality or how events are caused. In this view events are complexly interrelated. A particular event, say the selling of labor power, is determined by the nature of the exchange itself, as well as by any number of other events taking place in the economic, social, political, or cultural spheres. For example, authority relations within the production unit, gender relations within the family, the attitude of government towards unions, and cultural representations of labor in the larger society (e.g., how labor is portrayed in the media), all help to determine the terms on which labor power is sold. The process of hiring labor also plays a part in determining everything else. Marx viewed reality then as a rich totality of interpenetrating events and relationships.

Marx also saw social reality as constantly changing, as being in a constant state of flux. In the dialectical perspective, motion not rest characterizes the nature of the universe. Such motion results from the interpenetration of all social processes that create contradictory forces, pushing and pulling society in conflicting directions. For example, Marx identifies in capitalism the capital accumulation process as simultaneously a dynamic force unleashing the vast productive potential of technology while at the same time undermining itself by creating economic crises. The basis for such a contradiction will be discussed later on.

Not all contradictory tendencies are of importance to Marx, only those that are thought to be both necessary to the maintenance of a social process and destructive of that same process. This tension is the source of historical or social change. Dialectical inquiry then represents a dynamic view that allows for the identification of particular contradictory tendencies. The dynamic nature and contradictions of capitalism analyzed by Marx using the dialectical method will be discussed below.

The dialectical approach also embraces a particular epistemology. Knowledge is produced dialectically in this view by the act of inquiry in shaping reality as well as discovering knowledge. The process of theorizing is shaped by other social processes and shapes them in turn. Doing and thinking are fundamentally related to each other, forming a praxis. The production of knowledge is itself then a dynamic force influenced by the world as well as changing it. Marx sought to change the world with his ideas, and those who have followed in his intellectual footsteps continue to do so.

A related epistemological issue is Marx's conception of science. In the dialectical approach the goal of science is to locate the real essences of social processes by looking beyond the outward appearance of things. For example, Marx looked beyond the exchange of equivalents in labor markets (a truism he thought trivial) to the exploitation of labor that is hidden from sight by the outward appearance of market exchanges. By analyzing the labor market in the larger context of the capitalist-dominated production process, Marx shows how workers actually produce more value than they are paid. The dialectical approach tries to overcome, by emphasizing the relational, contradictory nature of the world, the many distortions which unconsciously affect our vision so that we are not deceived by appearances. The emphasis is on contexts, not "facts." Dialectics is an interpretive as well as empirical science. Although the main goal is not to generate empirically testable hypotheses, empirical verification has played and continues to play an important role in the Marxist tradition.

Historical Materialism

Historical materialism is Marx's distinctive conception of society and history.[2] Given the dialectical view that reality is a changing relational whole, where does one begin in his or her construction of knowledge? Marx's approach focuses on the material forces of society, that is, the concrete social existence of people as opposed to the realm of ideas. For Marx economic activities play a predominant role in shaping, or conditioning, both the individual and society.

Marx conceptually divides society into an economic base (substructure) and a noneconomic superstructure. These divisions are diagramed in Figure 1.1. The substructure of society consists of its mode of production, that is, the relations that people enter into in the process of producing and reproducing their means of

Figure 1.1 **Marx's Division of Society**

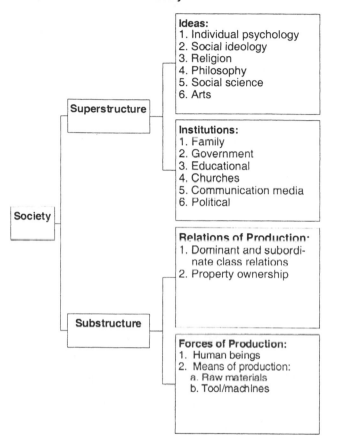

Ideas:
1. Individual psychology
2. Social ideology
3. Religion
4. Philosophy
5. Social science
6. Arts

Institutions:
1. Family
2. Government
3. Educational
4. Churches
5. Communication media
6. Political

Relations of Production:
1. Dominant and subordi-
   nate class relations
2. Property ownership

Forces of Production:
1. Human beings
2. Means of production:
   a. Raw materials
   b. Tool/machines

Superstructure

Society

Substructure

Source: Modified from Sherman (1987, 44).

subsistence, and the material conditions of production. Marx refers to the latter as the material forces of production, which include human beings (their skills, knowledge, needs), and the raw
materials and tools/machines referred to as the means of production. Human beings take raw materials from the natural environment and with the use of tools (instruments of production) reshape
or transform these natural objects into more useful products, and
as they do so they also shape themselves.

The relations that people enter into in the act of production Marx calls the social relations of production, which are definable in terms of control over the material forces of production. Marx observes that, except in tribal society, there have always been dominant classes able to exploit the labor of subordinate economic classes. This ability of one group to reap the fruits of others' labor is based, Marx thought, on control over the forces of production. Such control determines the economic class structure and nature of exploitation in society. For example, private ownership of the means of production gives the owning class a legal right to the social surplus, the portion of output that is produced by the nonowning class of workers, but appropriated by nonproducers. The mode of appropriation of the products of human labor, that is, the mode of exploitation, takes different forms, depending on the level of development of the material powers of production and on the particular property relationship (slave, feudal, capitalist). One of the fundamental problems Marx sought to explain was how labor was exploited under capitalist, or bourgeois, relations of production.

It is upon the material substructure of society that the rest of society—its legal, political, religious, aesthetic, and ideological elements, or superstructure—is built. These superstructural elements can take on the appearance of being independent social creations; once created they may follow a path of development divorced from the material circumstances in which they were born and may even influence the material substructure of society. Although the various aspects of society interact, for Marx the material base is the dominant, conditioning force and restricts the superstructural elements as independent forces.[3]

Marx saw history as a sequence of different modes of production, each representing "epochs marking progress in the economic development of society." Each succeeding mode represents a higher level of economic development that advances human and social development. The process of social change from one mode to another is based on the internal dynamics of contradictions existing within each mode of production; the seeds of self-destruction are also the seeds for a succeeding economic formation. Thus Roman society based on a slave mode of production gives way to European feudalism, and feudalism to capitalism.

In each socioeconomic formation conflicting forces exist. The basic conflict is between the material forces of society, which are seen as dynamic, and the relations of production, which are not. The source of antagonism between the social relations and the development of the material forces is divergent class interests. Social relations of production are resistant to change. Each mode of production advances the material development of society, but only within the limits of existing social relations of production. When the current relations of production block development of the material forces, the dominant classes who have vested interests in maintaining the status quo resist the required new relations of production.

The result is class conflict and struggle, which, according to Marx, act as a propelling force. The resolution of this conflict leads either to a new set of social relations of production, that is, new class relations and a new mode of production, or to the stagnation of society and the possible common ruin of the contending classes. The transition from one mode of production to another is not abrupt but unfolds over a long period of time. In Western Europe the transition from feudalism to capitalism took many years (1500–1800). During this historical period, the inherent contradictions of feudalism were heightened, and the ensuing class conflict and struggle led to the defeat of feudalism and the birth of capitalism. The growth of markets, the use of money in place of barter, the separation of town and country, the growth of a merchant class and moneylenders, the putting out system, although spawned by feudalism, were contradictory forces.

These contradictions placed a great strain on feudal relations of production, between lord and serf, and between the nobility and rising middle classes (merchants, money lenders, urban craft producers). The forces of change gradually dissolved feudalism, and slowly developed capitalism. By roughly 1800 early forms of capitalism had displaced feudalism in Western Europe, and the bourgeoisie had taken command of society from the feudal royalty and nobility. A revolution in the mode of production had taken place.

Marx thought that the capitalist relations of production would be the last antagonistic social form of production. Thereafter, production would come under the collective, democratic control of society and the interest of individuals would coincide with the community of interests.

Marx's Economic Analysis of Capitalism

For Marx the system-defining elements of any mode of production are the particular relations of production and the way surplus labor or product is extracted from the direct producers. One of the main tasks Marx set for himself was disclosing capitalist exploitation, which is obscured by complex exchange relationships among individuals and between classes.

Capitalist production is first of all characterized by the production of commodities, meaning here production for exchange rather than for use by the producers. Production takes place within a social structure wherein the laborer is denied control of the means of production, which are the private property of a small class of capitalists. Most people, who are property less and without means of production, must, for their survival, sell their labor power to those who own the means of production. In capitalism, labor power is thus reduced to a commodity bought and sold like any other commodity for a price (wages). Ownership of the means of production gives the capitalist the prerogative of buying labor power, and thus of managing both the laborer and the labor process. The sphere of production, and the class relations on which it is based, are the key focus of Marx's analysis of the exploitation process and the laws of motion of capitalism.

Surplus Extraction and Process of Exploitation

The prerequisite for such a system is that labor power be "free" to be bought and sold. Historically this meant the abolition of serfdom, which tied producers to the land and to feudal lords. It also meant forcibly separating the producers from their means of production and livelihood, so that they would be compelled to sell their labor power in order to live. Here the enclosure movement and laws against begging were instrumental in the creation of the proletariat. For Marx, there was little that was voluntary about this separation, and historically people resisted wage labor whenever they could. Marx wrote that "the working class comes into the world dripping from head to foot with blood."

These preconditions were established in the period of what Marx called the "primitive" or "original" accumulation of capital. For Marx capital is a social relation expressing the power of one class over another, rather than just a physical or technical relationship. Capital commands means of production and labor. The original accumulation of capital includes the creation of a proletariat ("conjuring whole populations out of the ground"), as well as the concentration of financial capital of sufficient size to command labor and the means of production. The state-chartered trading companies in the seventeenth and eighteenth centuries amassed large sums of financial capital. The means of production themselves must of course become commodities and the rise of the system of private property facilitates this. The primitive accumulation of capital corresponds to the mercantilist era of capitalism (1500–1800).

Marx viewed capitalism as a social system that conceals the real productive activities of society behind their commodity forms (land, labor, capital). The exchange of commodities between individuals obscures the class nature of capitalism, the origin of profit in surplus labor, and the exploitation of workers. Because capitalism produces commodities and because the "factors of production" are themselves commodities, all exchange appears not only as the relation of things but also as the exchange of equivalents.

However, capitalism is more than just a system of markets where commodities circulate, it is a system of production where commodities are produced. Production and circulation are treated as different moments in an organic whole; their unity becomes apparent through Marx's labor theory of value, which attempts to explain the causal links and interrelationships between production and circulation. Although Marx's labor theory of value is similar in some respects to Adam Smith and David Ricardo, Marx's theory is distinctive. Commodities have both a use value and an exchange value. Use value is determined by the specific and unique chemical/physical properties of each product. Exchange value, Marx argued, must be determined not by a commodity's use value, but by some common element embodied in all commodities that expressed the social nature of exchange. That common element was social labor. Commodities represent materialized human activity, and Marx argued that commodities were exchanged for each other in proportion to their labor content, taking into account both the direct labor used in production and indirect, past labor used to produce the tools, equipment, and other intermediate goods necessary to the production of commodities.

Only labor that is socially necessary creates value, determined by average conditions of productivity and social needs. For example, labor expended on the production of something no one wants to buy clearly produces no exchange value, nor does labor that takes twice as long on average to produce create more value than the labor of average productivity. Despite the fact that many different kinds of labor go into production, they are equated in the process of exchange. Marx accounted for these differences in the skills of labor by counting skilled labor as some multiple of simple labor. By applying the labor theory of value to capitalist production, Marx showed how workers are exploited and produce surplus value for capitalists. Capitalists start out with a sum of money and go into the market (sphere of circulation) to purchase raw material, tools, and equipment (constant capital) and labor power (variable capital). In the production process (sphere of production), labor power is transformed into labor that uses tools and equipment to work up raw materials into final products. The capitalist returns to the sphere of circulation and sells the final product for money, and if the capitalist is successful the sum of money at the end is larger than at the beginning, obtaining a profit.

Marx calls this metamorphosis the circuit of capital, where capital changes form from money capital to productive capital to commodity capital and then back again into money capital. The circuit of capital is diagramed below:

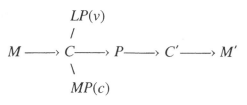

$$LP(v)$$
$$/$$
$$M \longrightarrow C \longrightarrow P \longrightarrow C' \longrightarrow M'$$
$$\backslash$$
$$MP(c)$$

Circulation	Production	Circulation
Money-capital phase	Productive-capital phase	Commodity-capital phase

The circuit shows capital starting out as money in the sphere of circulation (market), then in the form of productive capital entering the sphere of production, and finally reentering the sphere of circulation (market) in its commodity capital form where it transforms itself back into money capital its original form. The difference between M' and M represents the capitalists profit.

The source of this profit is surplus value (the difference between the value of C and the value C') produced by labor in the production process. Marx argued that the profits of the industrial capitalist came from the exploitation of workers who produced more value for the capitalist than the value of their labor power. The total value of production (TP) is determined in part by the amount of raw materials used and tools/equipment used up (depreciation). Marx called this constant capital (c) its value equal to the amount of previous labor time that it took to produce. It is constant because it is only capable of transferring its value to the commodity it is currently being used to produce. The second part of total value is the value of labor power (v). Here, unlike Smith and Ricardo, Marx applies the labor theory of value to determine its value. The value of labor power is equal to the labor that it takes to produce the bundle of goods that makes up the workers' standard of living, that is, what it takes to physically and culturally reproduce the worker. Marx assumed that the capitalist bought means of production and labor power at prices and wages equal to their values. If true, then the source of capitalist profit is not unequal exchange. Buying cheap and selling dear is the source of merchants' profit, but not the industrial capitalist.

Profits are produced and exploitation takes place not in the sphere of circulation but in production, where capitalists convert labor power purchased into actual work or labor. Here workers are compelled to produce surplus value(s), that is, they produce more value than they are paid for. If it takes an average worker eight hours to produce a value equivalent to the value of her labor power (equal to the wage), but this worker is compelled to work a sixteen-hour day (not uncommon in Marx's day), then this worker is producing surplus value during the extra eight hours. Marx called this extra time surplus labor. Surplus labor is part of the necessary labor time that it takes to produce a commodity, but the worker is not paid for the value produced during this time. The capitalist appropriates surplus value.

The total value of production is:

$$TP = c + v + s$$

where:

c = value of means of production used up
v = value of labor power = wages
s = surplus value = surplus labor

and

$$v + s = \text{necessary labor}$$

In terms of the circuit of capital:

$$C = c + v$$
$$C' = c + v + s$$

and

$$M' - M = \text{surplus value} = C' - C$$

The circuit of capital does not end here. The capitalist must invest a portion of the newly created surplus value in new means of production and labor power or else be driven out of business by competitors. This driving force behind the capitalist exerts itself as an external, objective force (independent of any subjective motives of the capitalist) over which the capitalist has little control. Only by constantly extending his capital and by "revolutionizing" the means of production can the capitalist preserve his capital in the competitive struggle for profits. The process where capital reproduces not only itself but produces surplus value is referred to by Marx as the expanded reproduction of capital, or simply capital accumulation.

The Laws of Motion of Capitalism

The dynamics of capitalist commodity production, what Marx called the "laws of motion" of capitalism, are derived from an analysis of the capital accumulation process. First, Marx's analysis captures the power of capitalism to rapidly transform and develop the material forces of production industrializing society. Marx writes eloquently about capitalism's progressive qualities:

> during its rule of scarce one hundred years, [capitalism] has created more massive and more colossal productive forces than have all preceding generations together. Subjection of nature's forces to man, machinery, application of chemistry to industry and agriculture, steam-navigation, railways, electric telegraphs, clearing whole continents for cultivation, canalization of rivers, whole populations conjured out of the ground—what earlier century had even a presentiment that such productive forces slumbered in the labor of social labor? (Marx, *Communist Manifesto*, pp. 13–14)

Although Marx's analysis reveals the tremendous growth-producing tendency of capitalism, his analysis also reveals the contradictory nature of capitalism's laws of motion. Marx identifies several contradictions:

1. *Concentration and Centralization of Capital:* The accumulation process has a tendency to concentrate individual capital into larger and larger enterprises utilizing massive means of production. Competition also produces a tendency for capital to centralize into fewer and fewer hands as stronger firms drive weaker firms out of the market and/or absorb them through merger. The concentration and centralization of capital is a law of motion of capitalism that on the one hand produces the powerful growth tendency within capitalism, and on the other hand underlies the contradictory effects of foreign expansion, economic crises, and inequality discussed below.

2. *Foreign Expansion:* The incessant search for profits, prompted by competition, drives capitalists beyond the boundaries of their own countries in the search for foreign markets, cheap raw materials, and labor. While Marx thought this would spread the development of capitalism to the rest of the world, it also produced colonialism and imperialism. Although Marx's analysis of this contradiction was very incomplete, later Marxists (Vladimir Lenin, Rosa Luxemburg, Rudolf Hilferding, and Nikolai Bukharin) expanded Marx's analysis of imperialism. [For discussion of these early Marxists see Barone 1985, ch. 2.]

3. *Economic Crises:* Capitalism is inherently unstable, characterized by boom and bust. Marx analyzed four tendencies that produced economic crisis. First, as capitalism developed it uses more and more machinery relative to labor. Marx called this a rising organic composition of capital. Given that labor is the sole source of surplus value, a rising organic composition of capital makes it increasingly more difficult to maintain the rate of profit. Thus Marx argued there was a tendency in capitalism for the rate of profit to fall. A falling rate of profit induces capitalists to cut back. An economic crisis ensues unless the falling rate of profit can be offset by strategies to increase the rate of profit such as foreign expansion or increasing the rate of exploitation.

The second cause of crisis was a tendency for capital to accumulate too fast relative to the purchasing power of workers. This tendency comes from capitalists overinvesting (overproduction) and from the restricted wages of workers (underconsumption). Finding themselves with excess productive capacity (and lower profits) capitalists cut back, producing an economic crisis. The crisis restores the balance between production and consumption by eliminating capacity as weaker firms close their doors.

The third tendency underlying economic crises is what Marx called disproportionality. The market as a coordinating mechanism does not always work out smoothly and quickly to eliminate market shortages and surpluses. This can cause disruptions (shortages and bottlenecks) in the accumulation process and has the potential if they occur in key sectors of the economy to bring about a general decline.

4. *Reserve Army of Unemployed:* The fourth cause of economic crises is singled out as a contradiction in its own right given the importance Marx attached it. Put simply, Marx argued that unemployment is a permanent feature of capitalism, necessary to the profitable accumulation of capital. In a period of expansion, capitalists draw down on the reserve army, diminishing its ranks. This improves the bargaining power of workers who are now able to get higher wages from their employers. Higher wages mean less profit for capitalists, who may either cut back production or adopt labor-saving technologies in response to lower rates of profit. In either case, workers will be fired, replenishing the reserve army of workers, eliminating the upward pressure on wages, and restoring capitalists' profits.

5. *Increasing Misery of the Proletariat:* Despite the great wealth-producing capabilities of capitalism, this is offset by a tremendous degree of inequality and impoverishment for many. Marx argued that capitalism would create a permanent underclass of poor people who were no longer needed for profitable accumulation. Additionally, the cyclical nature of the accumulation process meant that workers frequently would be laid off, plunging them into poverty. Marx called this the absolute impoverishment of the working class. Although Marx thought real wages could increase (but not without class struggle), such increases would always lag behind the growth of capitalist wealth. Marx called this the relative

impoverishment of the working class. Thus Marx thought that the benefits of capitalism would be very unequally shared, keeping many impoverished.

6. *Alienation:* Marx also thought that people would increasingly experience social and psychological deformation (alienation) under capitalism. Workers are alienated from the product of their labor, which becomes the property of another. Part of their product (surplus value) comes back in the form of means of production such as the assembly line, where workers are more like slaves to machines than controllers. Private ownership of the means of production places control over production and the labor process with the owners of capital. Workers become just another input, a means to others' ends, alienated from the process of production. The capitalist division of labor consigns to workers progressively more boring, repetitious, mindless jobs. Capitalist treatment of workers is harsh and conditions of work dangerous and oppressive. Additionally, people's lives are subject to blind capitalist market forces, leaving people with little control over their economic destiny.

Despite the high level of interdependence there are few opportunities for workers to cooperate with each other and feel solidarity with others. Workers are ranked, ordered, and become part of large-scale hierarchical (bureaucratic) orders as capital becomes more concentrated and centralized. With a large reserve army of unemployed, workers must compete for scare jobs. Workers are thus alienated from each other in these highly competitive, stratified orders inherent in capitalism.

Finally, Marx argued that workers were alienated from their own human essence under capitalism with few opportunities to develop their full human potential to lead full and enriched lives. Capitalists too were alienated according to Marx, separated from the majority of humanity and from their real human essence by their capitalist role.

Marx did not limit his view of human potential to economic man or woman; in fact, his view extended well beyond materialism to embrace a rich cultural being that included our artistic, intellectual, and spiritual abilities.

7. *Effective Socialization of Production:* Marx thought that as capitalism developed it became more and more social with the advancing division of labor, the rise of large-scale production, and internationalization of capital. The fragmentation of earlier patriarchal, slave, or feudal arrangements became progressively transformed by capitalism, where the work of each was indispensable to the survival of all. This growing social nature would increasingly conflict with the private nature of capitalist ownership and distribution, that is, the forces of production conflict with the existing relations of production. While the increasingly social nature of production and distribution begs for social control and regulation according to a conscious social plan, the blind forces of the market govern it, by variations in the rate of profit subject to all the contradictions discussed above. It was Marx's analysis of this ultimate contradiction that led him to predict that socialism would be the logical next step after capitalism had exhausted its progressive potential.[4]

In summary, Marx's laws of motion of capitalism are derived utilizing a dialectical and historical materialist approach. His analysis of capitalism focuses on class, exploitation, and the process of capital accumulation. Capitalism's inherent need to expand brings more and more constant as well as variable capital under its sway, as it expands into every branch of production and every region of the world, confronting an ever-greater proportion of the population as an objective and subjective power over the labor process. Although capitalism represents a progressive step forward in social evolution, its contradictions limit its historical role in social development.

The Demise of Capitalism and the Rise of Socialism

Although Marx was very clearly morally opposed to capitalist society and sought to overthrow it, his prediction that capitalism would fall and socialism/communism rise was based on his analysis of capitalism and the laws of motion of human history (historical materialism). The contradictions that Marx identifies in capitalism offset to a significant degree and limit capitalism's growth-producing potential. Marx thought that these contradictions would heighten and intensify as capitalism developed over time, spreading the seeds of its own destruction just as had earlier modes of production such as feudalism. Those very same relations would at some point block the tremendous advance in the material forces of production brought about by capitalist relations of production.

Riddled with problems, generated by the very success of capitalism, the forces of change would be set in motion. Marx thought class conflict would spread and a proletarian revolution take place. People would become increasingly conscious of the true nature of capitalism and the need to replace capitalism with a nonexploitative system that substituted social, democratic control over the forces of production for private capitalist control; that substituted social needs for private profit; and that substituted rational social planning for blind market forces. This new social system, which Marx called socialism, would be a stepping stone toward a classless society—communism—characterized by egalitarianism, solidarity, and community.[5] It would be a society of freely associated individuals working with means of production held in common and having a definite social plan. It would be a society where the full and free development of each is the condition for the development of all. Human relations would be direct and not perverted by money and market relations. There would be a complete emancipation of all human senses and qualities.

Socialism/communism would mean the overthrow of all social relationships where people are humbled, enslaved, abandoned, or otherwise oppressed as under capitalism. The goal of this new society, according to Marx, is the full development of human beings: the free unfolding of their human powers; the full realization of their potentials in all their dimensions including the capacity for love; and the achievement of the rational regulation of their natural and social environment.

The problems (contradictions) generated by capitalism then are solvable, according to Marx, only by a complete transformation of society, by a revolution in the mode of production. Capitalism is a stage in the history of human and social development driven by the human desire to achieve one's full human potential. Capitalism unleashes the human productive potential, but in the process limits the full utilization of that potential in ways that promote the development of the full range of human capabilities. Once reaching the limits of its historically progressive role, capitalism would be succeeded by socialism/communism.

Those who followed in Marx's intellectual and political footsteps have built upon a very rich intellectual foundation. It is this intellectual tradition that inspired and informed the ideas of radical political economy in the post World War II period. Marx's ideas will be evident in the theory of radical political economy discussed in the next chapter.

Notes

1. For a more extended discussion of dialectics, see Heilbroner (1980, ch. 2), and Resnick and Wolff (1987, chs. 1–2), from which this account is largely drawn.

2. For a more in-depth discussion of historical materialism, see Gurley (1979, ch. 2), from which this account is largely drawn.

3. The exact relationship posited by Marx between the base and superstructure has been the subject of much debate among Marxists. For two conflicting views, see Cohen (1978) and Resnick and Wolff (1987).

4. This discussion is drawn from Mandel (1962 vol. 1, 170–171).

5. The following discussion of socialism/communism is drawn from Gurley (1979, 58–61).

References

Baran, Paul. 1957. *The Political Economy of Growth.* New York: Monthly Review Press.

Baran, Paul, and Paul Sweezy. 1966. *Monopoly Capital.* New York: Monthly Review Press.

Barone, Charles. 1985. *Marxist Thought on Imperialism.* Armonk, NY: M.E. Sharpe.

Cohen, G.A. 1978. *Karl Marx's Theory of History: A Defense.* London: Oxford University Press.

Frank, Andre Gunder. 1967. *Capitalism and Underdevelopment.* New York: Monthly Review Press.

Gurley, John. 1979. *Challengers to Capitalism: Marx, Lenin, Stalin, Mao.* 2d ed. New York: Norton.

Heilbroner, Robert L. 1980. *Marxism For and Against.* New York: Norton, 1980.

Magdoff, Harry. 1968. *The Age of Imperialism.* New York: Monthly Review Press.

Mandel, Ernest. 1962. *Marxist Economic Theory.* Vols I and II. New York: Monthly Review Press.

Marx, Karl. 1998. *Communist Manifesto: a Modern Edition.* Reprint ed. New York: Verso.

Resnick, Stephen A., and Richard D. Wolff. 1987. *Knowledge and Class.* Chicago: University of Chicago Press.

Sherman, Howard. 1987. *Foundations of Radical Political Economy.* Armonk, NY: M.E. Sharpe.

Sweezy, Paul. 1942. *Theory of Capitalist Development.* New York: Monthly Review Press.

Further Reading

Books About Marx

Elliot, John E. 1981. *Marx and Engels on Economics, Politics, and Society: Essential Readings with Editorial Commentary.* Santa Monica, CA: Goodyear Publishing.

Fromm, Erich. 1961. *Marx's Concept of Man.* New York: Frederick Ungar.

Gurley, John. 1979. *Challengers to Capitalism: Marx, Lenin, Stalin, Mao.* 2d ed. New York: Norton.

Heilbroner, Robert L. 1980. *Marxism For and Against.* New York: Norton, 1980.

Howard, M.C., and J.E. King. 1988. *The Political Economy of Marx.* 2d ed. New York: New York University Press.

Mandel, Ernest. 1962. *Marxist Economic Theory.* Vols I and II. New York: Monthly Review Press.

Resnick, Stephen A., and Richard D. Wolff. 1987. *Knowledge and Class.* Chicago: University of Chicago Press.

Sweezy, Paul. 1942. *Theory of Capitalist Development.* New York: Monthly Review Press.

Weeks, John. 1981. *Capital and Exploitation.* Princeton, NJ: Princeton University Press.

Works by Marx

For a complete list of the writing of Marx (and Engels), many of which can be downloaded free of charge, go to: www.marxists.org/archive/marx/works/.

Radical Journals

Against the Current
Antipode: A Radical Journal of Geography
Cambridge Journal of Economics
Capital and Class
Capitalism, Nature, and Socialism
Critical Sociology (Previously *The Insurgent Sociologist*)
Dissent
Dollars and Sense
Kapitalistate
Latin American Perspectives
Monthly Review
New Left Review
Politics and Society
Radical History Review
Rethinking Marxism
Review of Radical Political Economics
Science and Society
Socialist Review
Z Magazine

2 METHOD, CORE CONCEPTS, AND CAPITALISM

Radical political economy (RPE) consists of a particular methodology, theoretical analysis of capitalism, and vision for the future. The broad contours of Marx's ideas will be evident in what follows, yet RPE has extended and modified Marx, reflecting the changes that have taken place since the nineteenth century in the development of capitalism and in the way we understand the world.

Although there are several different strands of radical economic thought and there is considerable debate over methodological and theoretical issues among radicals, these differences and debates will for the most part be ignored here. Instead a synthetic view that brings together contributions from several strands of RPE will be utilized. Such a task of course runs the risk of offending everyone and doing justice to no one. However, the intention here is to introduce people to the radical way of thinking, not to provide a definitive text on the various nuances and complexities of RPE. (For a useful delineation of the differences among radicals, see Roberts and Feiner, Introduction).

The presentation of RPE begins with a discussion of methodology and the core concepts of surplus product and class. This chapter is drawn in part from Bowles and Edwards (1993, chs. 1–7).

Radical Approach to Economics

Radicals define economics as *the study of the labor processes that produce the goods and services, and reproduce the people and social relations necessary to sustain life and society.* An economic system is a set of relationships among people, a way of organizing the labor processes, including how work is done, what work is done, and how the resulting outputs are distributed and used.

In RPE the economic system includes more than just the production of things, it also includes the production and reproduction of people and social relations, that is, people are both inputs and outputs in this view. People are shaped and molded by their labor-process experiences, by the social relations and culture of the workplace. (For a discussion of these relationships, see Hahnel 1981, 65–92 and Burawoy 1982.) Additionally, the labor process is not limited to the economic system but includes the reproduction of people both biologically and culturally in homes, schools, churches, as well as in offices and factories. The emphasis is on people and their social relations with each other. Different economic systems organize these relationships in different ways.

In the radical view, economic systems do not exist in isolation from the rest of society. They are fundamentally interrelated with political, social, and larger cultural systems. The shaded overlapping areas in Figure 2.1 represent the interrelatedness of the different aspects of society. For example, patriarchy as a cultural symbolic system plays an important part in insuring male dominance at the workplace as well as in the home. Likewise, the distribution of economic assets has a profound effect on political processes and outcomes. The labor processes in production and reproduction are viewed as indispensable parts of an economic system and the larger society that surrounds it. Society is treated as an interrelated whole.

The radical approach to studying economic systems has been characterized as three-dimensional: a horizontal dimension (competition), a vertical dimension (command), and a time dimension (change). The horizontal dimension includes those relationships

Figure 2.1 **Holistic View of Society**

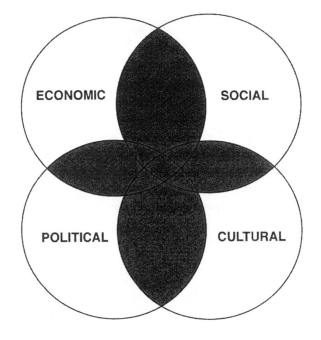

that are for the most part voluntary, where relative equality of power exists, and competition obtains. Many market or exchange relationships in capitalism fit this definition. Buyers and sellers compete with each other as they exercise their choices in the marketplace. The horizontal dimension can also be applied to noneconomic relationships such as the political election process, which in part fits this definition. The horizontal dimension then refers to relationships, both economic and noneconomic, that can be characterized as competitive and voluntary.

The vertical or command dimension includes all relationships in which power, coercion, and hierarchy play the predominant role. Power is used to command others and shape or condition the choices of others (here the horizontal and vertical dimensions overlap). In capitalism domination and subordination are central aspects of society: it exists in the workplace as well as in the household, government, and pervades the relations of different classes, races, and sexes. As we will see, RPE places great emphasis on the command dimension of the economic system.

The third dimension includes time or change and tries to capture the dynamic nature of economic systems; the way the operation of the economy changes the system itself. All economic systems have a history and how an economic system performs at any particular time depends in part on its history. The future of any economic system is also in part determined by changes taking place in the present. The history of capitalism from the nineteenth century to the present is replete with dramatic changes in technology, in the kinds of products produced, in the process of work, as well as how we live, where we live, and the very shape of our communities. RPE tries to capture this dimension of capitalism, to explain the process of change over time.

Competition, command, and change are ways then in which radicals characterize the relationships within an economic system. This defines the particular approach and way of ordering (or simplifying) society that radicals use to focus on what they see as important economic relations.

The final aspect of the RPE methodology is its value orientation. Like most social scientists, radicals are interested in evaluating how well or badly society works as well as understanding how it works. Evaluating the performance of any part of society including the economy requires a set of evaluating principles. Such principles or values not only provide a standard by which to measure performance, they also influence the choice of what one finds important and unimportant to look at. The three dimensions of RPE discussed above reflect such a value choice.

There are four core values underlying RPE: economic efficiency, quality of life, equality, and democracy:

1. Economic efficiency as an evaluative principle or value means more to radicals than just getting the most output from a given set of inputs. First, radicals are concerned with goods and services that are useful and satisfy real human needs. Advertising, military goods, and needless style changes are examples of products and

services that are wasteful and thus represent inefficient use of resources. Second, radicals are concerned with all inputs including the natural environment, health of workers, and household labor. Radicals place a high value on conserving these and other inputs. To the extent that our economic system abuses or ignores the value of these inputs, there is an inefficient use of resources.

2. Quality of life includes worker job satisfaction, and the quality of family and social life. A high value is placed by radicals on the psychological well-being of workers. Work should be intrinsically satisfying and consistent with the goal of allowing individuals to realize their full human capabilities. If jobs are repetitious and boring, then this is seen as stultifying and injurious to workers' well-being. If the pace of work or the length of the workday leaves workers unable to participate fully in family life or to enjoy leisure, this is viewed as detrimental to the well-being of workers and their families.

The quality of life also includes the quality of community life. Does the economy provide an adequate material base for healthy community life? Does the economy provide the necessary stability for enduring community relations? If the economy works in ways that are destructive of community life, then the economic system is viewed as deficient. Although quality of life and economic efficiency are not always in conflict, when they are radicals are usually unwilling to sacrifice the well-being of workers and the quality of community life in favor of economic efficiency.

3. Equality means that the burdens and benefits generated by the economic system are shared equitably. For radicals there is a general presumption of equality unless circumstances (e.g., family size) or democratic decisions in which everyone has an equal say determine otherwise. An economic system that shares its burdens and benefits more equally than another is a better one in this view. Radicals, therefore, are highly egalitarian. In the radical view, unequal burden and benefit sharing largely results from exploitation.

4. The fourth value held by radicals is the degree to which the economic system promotes democracy. Democracy means that

decision-making power is accountable to those who are affected; that civil rights and personal liberties exist; and that people have relatively equal access to political resources and influences. Radicals are concerned with the degree to which the economic system promotes or retards political democracy as well as how much the economic system fosters democracy in other spheres of society, including the economy itself.

All decisions that affect more than one person should, in the radical view, be subject to democratic processes that entitle those affected to have a say in making the decision. For example, the corporate owners' decision to close down a plant affecting workers and the community is considered inappropriate by radicals because it is undemocratic. Democracy and command are not necessarily in conflict as long as the command decision is arrived at democratically, such as the enforcement of democratically created environmental protection laws. Radicals thus place a very high value on democracy in all areas of life. This commitment to democracy by radicals is the basis of powerful critiques of both capitalism and the "socialism" that existed in countries like the USSR, issues that will be taken up in chapter 6.

These four values—efficiency, quality of life, equality, and democracy—both inform the theory of RPE and provide the evaluative criteria that are used by radicals to evaluate the performance of an economic system.

Core Concepts: Surplus Product and Class

Surplus product is a key theoretical concept for radicals and is the basis for their theoretical analysis of the vertical or command dimension of the economic system. The economy produces a certain amount of goods and services or total product each year. If we subtract from total product the necessary product, the amount of goods and services needed to maintain or replace the inputs used up (workers, tools, and raw materials), what remains is surplus product.

There are two components of the necessary product. The first component is the amount of goods and services required to replace the raw materials and capital goods used up in production. By subtracting from the total product just the replacement of raw materials and capital goods used (depreciation), we are left with what is widely referred to as the Net Product.

The second component is made up of the goods and services necessary to maintain the producers at their customary or traditional standard of living (necessary consumption). This includes consumption necessary to restore the workers' energies after a day's work, to reproduce the next generation of workers who will replace those who retire, and to maintain those who are retired from the workforce. Necessary consumption should not be confused with biological and subsistence minimums. The level of necessary consumption can be high or low depending upon labor productivity, labor intensity, the length of the workday, as well as what is considered customary within particular cultures. This varies a great deal historically and cross culturally.

Summarizing this information we have:

TOTAL PRODUCT
minus Raw Materials and Depreciation
NET PRODUCT
minus Necessary Consumption
SURPLUS PRODUCT

The total amount of labor time spent each year producing the total product is divided between producing the necessary product—necessary to replace all the inputs human and material used in the production process—and the surplus product.

Let us apply this concept first to a non-surplus-producing society where the necessary product exhausts the annual total product. In this society only enough is produced to replace the raw materials and capital goods used up, and to provide for the necessary consumption of the producers. At the end of the year the community is no better or worse off than it was before. Just enough has been produced to reproduce the workers at their customary standard of living and replace the raw materials and worn-out capital goods. In this society there is no surplus product, and no surplus labor was performed. Such a society might be characterized economically as stagnant or steady state, depending upon whether or not the outcome was viewed as desirable.

Now let us assume a new technology has been discovered which allows this society to produce a larger total product so that after we subtract the necessary product, a surplus product remains. The existence of a surplus creates new options for this society. For example, the surplus could be used to increase next year's production by expanding the stock of capital goods and using more workers. By doing this every year, a society would be able to experience economic growth and expanded reproduction. Alternatively, it could use the surplus to increase necessary consumption of all or part of the people, or it might decide to cut back on the number of hours worked next time around and increase leisure time.

For radicals, the most important change associated with the production of surplus product, aside from the potential for economic growth, is the possibility it creates for particular groups in society to avoid permanently productive work. A surplus product creates an opportunity for nonproducers to consume without doing productive work.

Of course children and the elderly in industrialized economies usually consume without doing productive work. However, radicals are more concerned with those who never have and never will have to do any productive work. These groups can be divided into two groups: exploitative and nonexploitative. The latter group includes spiritual leaders, warriors, and others who serve in various capacities at the request of their communities.

Exploitative groups are those that are able to force or otherwise coerce the producers to turn their surplus over to them. It is only when a society's labor productivity has advanced to the point where a surplus is produced, that the possibility for systematic economic exploitation exists. An economic system based on such exploitation is called a class society. Classes exist in all societies where those who produce the total product (including the surplus product) and those who control the surplus are separate groups. This includes slave, feudal, sharecropping, capitalist, and even state socialist societies such as those found in China or in the Soviet Union from 1917 to 1989.

Class and class relations in RPE are the principal aspects of the vertical command dimension of the economy. A class is a group that shares a common position in the economy. For radicals that position is defined quite precisely in terms of production and control of the means of production. There are three important elements of the radical definition of class. First, class is a relational concept. For a class to exist there has to be another class in relationship with it. For example, you cannot have a slave-owning class without a class of slaves.

Second, class relations are defined by particular positions within the labor process, not by status, social esteem, or income level. Although these are clearly relative to one's class position they do not in the radical view determine class position. In a slave-owning society, the ownership of the direct producers gives the slave owner control over the labor process. Likewise, in a capitalist society ownership of the means of production gives owners control over workers and their labor process. It is a group's position relative to the labor process that defines its class relation.

Here we can see quite clearly the third element of the radical definition of class, its hierarchical nature. Class refers to a group on top and a group on the bottom. The class on top is in a command position over the one on the bottom. For a class to be a surplus receiver, as opposed to surplus producer, it must have control over the labor process of others, it must be able to compel others to work, and it must have some claim to the output of the labor process.

Economic Systems and Capitalism

We can begin applying these key concepts of RPE to understand economic systems in general and capitalism in particular. Each economic system has a different class structure and organization, a distinctive way of organizing the labor process and controlling the economic surplus. Class structures and organization are usually enforced by a society's legal code expressed in terms of property rights. For example, in a slave society, slave owners have a legal right to control the labor process of the slave and the right to the output produced by the slave (and thus surplus product). The slave owner also has a legal right to any children produced by the slave. These legal rights, conferred upon the slave owner, come from property rights associated with private ownership of the producers who are slaves.

Under feudalism serfs tilled the land and were obligated to turn over a proportion of the output (surplus product) to lords. This initially took the form of in-kind payments and later (around 1500) was transmuted into money rents and other fees charged by the lords. In addition, serfs were often obligated to provide labor dues, that is, unpaid domestic labor performed in the lord's household. The surplus product allowed the lords to support themselves luxuriously, build castles and cathedrals, finance their Crusades, and lead noble lifestyles generally.

The lords had a legal right to the surplus product and surplus labor even though the serfs were not slaves, even though there were no private property rights in land, and even though the labor process was for the most part controlled and organized by the serfs. Serfs were legally tied to the land and were not free to move. The courts based on feudal property rights legally enforced these obligations. Ultimately, the power of the lords was based on the military might of the lords to punish anyone who refused to turn over part of his or her output, provide labor dues, or tried to leave the lord's manor.

Capitalism too has a distinctive class structure and organization, although its class basis is perhaps less transparent than the class basis of slavery and feudalism. Nonetheless, capitalism is a system of domination and subordination. Commodities are produced for profit using privately owned capital goods and wage labor. The surplus product accrues to the capitalist in the form of profits. There are five distinctive features of capitalism in RPE:

1   Generalized commodity production and markets.
2   Private ownership of the means of production (capital goods).
3   Wage labor.
4   Production for profit.
5   Patriarchy and white racism.

Capitalism is historically the first economic system where commodity production is generalized. In precapitalist societies production was mostly for use rather than exchange. In capitalism most products are produced for exchange, although there are significant exceptions such as the household sphere where the products and services of household labor (performed mostly women) are not exchanged directly for money in a market. Under capitalism even the means of production and labor are commodities and are in an economic sense produced (or reproduced) for exchange.

The market is the basic mechanism through which exchanges are facilitated in capitalism. Markets regulate and coordinate commodity exchanges through price movements caused by supply and demand conditions in markets for means of production, labor power, and final goods and services. Although markets are the primary exchange-regulating mechanism, other regulating mechanisms exist in capitalism such as government regulation and planning, for example, price controls, industrial policy, and regulation (and outright prohibition) of the sale of certain goods. The extent of such non-market-regulating mechanisms varies within capitalism and is according to radicals dependent upon the needs of capitalist accumulation and the strength of various classes to translate their interests politically into public policy. This aspect of RPE will be discussed more fully in the next chapter.

Private ownership of the means of production places most of the land, raw materials, tools, equipment, and factories in the hands of individuals who are free to dispose of this property (sell, use, or withhold it) as they see fit. Exceptions to private ownership include public or government ownership that has a very limited place in capitalism, especially in the United States.

Radicals distinguish between independent and dependent commodity production. Independent commodity production is where individuals or families own their tools of production as well as their workplaces. They produce commodities with their own labor and sell them in the market as commodities. Freeholders and guild producers during the Middle Ages are examples of independent commodity producers. The colonial period in the United States was also characterized by independent commodity production. Although independent commodity production (e.g., family farms today) can co-exist with capitalism, radicals point out that in the United States it has declined over the last 200 years from about 80 percent to 17 percent of commodity production (Bowles and Edwards 1993, ch. 1).[1]

Most production in capitalism takes the form of dependent commodity production where one group (a distinct minority) owns the means of production and another group (a majority) provides the labor in the form of wage labor, the third characteristic of capitalism in the radical definition. Those who do not own the means of production must sell their labor power to those who do own the means of production. In exchange for a wage these laborers work for the owners of the means of production. Thus wage labor and private ownership of capital goods are closely related in capitalism. Although wage labor has an element of voluntary exchange (horizontal dimension), workers are in a position of structural inequality (vertical dimension). Those who do not own capital usually have to work for those who do in order to survive.

Unlike conventional economists, radicals argue that profits in capitalism result from class structure, the vertical dimension of capitalism, not markets. Capitalist profits alone determine whether production will occur. Control over the labor process (and wage laborers) by employers (capitalists) entitles the capitalist to the surplus product produced by labor. Capitalists hire workers to produce output, output which the capitalist owns. Out of the total revenue obtained from the sale of the output, capitalists pay wages sufficient for the workers customary standard of living and set aside enough to replace the materials and means of production used up. The remaining revenue is profit, the form that surplus product takes in capitalism. Some of this profit ends up being shared with moneylenders and other groups.[2]

Capitalists and workers thus constitute separate classes in capitalism. Capitalists own the capital goods used in production and as a result control the labor of others, the labor process, and the surplus product. The working class consists of those who do not own capital goods and perform wage labor. Workers produce the total product, but have little control over the labor of others or the labor process. They are surplus producers not surplus receivers. Like other class-based economic systems, the class structure of capitalism is relational, related to the labor process, and hierarchical. Although much of RPE is based on this two-class model, other classes are recognized and will be discussed later in this chapter.

In addition to class domination, radicals also identify two other systems of domination associated with capitalism: patriarchy and white racism. Although these forms of discrimination and oppression preceded the development of capitalism, they have carried over into capitalism and have been integrated into the class system in ways that reinforce each other. Capitalism strengthens patriarchy by keeping women economically dependent upon men (husbands), while patriarchy strengthens capitalism by providing a large pool of unpaid and low-paid female labor. Similarly white racism divides workers, preventing class unity, thus enhancing capitalist power and control, while lower wages and higher unemployment for nonwhites perpetuate racist stereotypes on which racial domination is based.

Thus while class and class relations are central to the vertical dimension of RPE, other relations of domination are also important aspects of command in the economic system. The importance of race and gender in capitalism will be discussed more fully in the next two chapters.

Accumulation and Change in Capitalism

Competition (horizontal dimension) among capitalists for profits produces powerful forces for change (time dimension) in capitalism. The separation of producers from their means of production and the separation of individual owners of the means of production from each other enforces competition that compels capitalists to reinvest their profits (surplus product). The continuous reinvestment of surplus over time in search of profits is called capital accumulation in RPE.

The capital accumulation process includes mobilizing, transforming, and exploiting the inputs used in capitalist production and marketing. Transforming the labor process, generating new supplies of labor and raw materials, and increasing the stock of capital goods are all parts of this process. The accumulation process is the basic source of change in capitalism. Capitalists create change by investing profits and they change the world in order to make more profits.

So powerful are these forces of change, that capitalism has in a relatively short period of time radically transformed the very fabric of society and the world. Wherever the capital accumulation process has been self-sustaining, capitalism has very quickly become the dominant economic system, either by driving other forms of production (e.g., feudal) into extinction or by harnessing (e.g., family farms) these forms in a social formation where capitalist production predominates.

Capitalist development has been characterized by rapid population growth, migration of millions of people, urbanization, and continuous scientific and technological breakthroughs in production, in land and sea transportation, and in communication. Real incomes have increased, and people's diets, housing, and lifestyles have changed dramatically. The sources of people's incomes changed from agriculture to industry. Independent commodity production was replaced by dependent production and people began working for someone else. Capitalism also introduced workers to the dangers of industrial work as well as the insecurity and material hardships of unemployment. Social and family life also have been radically transformed with the development of the nuclear family, the greatly reduced capacity of the family as a production unit, and the geographical separation of kin groups.

From its original European and British centers of accumulation, capitalism has since the 1500s grown and spread throughout much of the world. However, the rate of capitalist change has been uneven and the nature of social change different depending upon time and place. For example, the impact of the spread of capitalism into the Third World has been very different from the impact of capitalism in England or the United States. According to radicals, capitalism has ravaged the Third World, leaving mass poverty and underdevelopment in its wake. This will be discussed more fully in a discussion of imperialism in chapter 5.

U.S. Capitalism

The growth and development of capitalism in the United States over the last 200 years has caused many profound changes. In the late 1700s capitalist relations (dependent commodity production) accounted for no more than 6 percent of the economically active population in the United States. Home production, independent commodity production, slavery, and Native American communal/kinship production were the predominant relations of production.

The growth of capitalist relations gradually forced those using noncapitalist methods to choose between adopting capitalist relations (and uncertain success) or certain economic ruin in competition with cheaper capitalist production. For most (especially white males) the alternative was wage labor, even though many were willing to endure individual/family hardship rather than tolerate wage labor. The supply of wage laborers also came from large numbers of immigrants who had little or no wealth and were thus forced into wage employment.

The dream of being ones own boss, an independent commodity producer, or businessperson continues to define the aspirations of many "USers"* today, even though the opportunities for realizing

---

*This term will be used to denote those living in the United States instead of the more usual "Americans" which although appropriated by the people of the United States to refer only to them could also legitimately be used to refer to those who live elsewhere in North America, Central America, and South America.

Table 2.1

Class Control

	Owns capital goods used in production?	
	Yes	No
Controls the labor of others?		
Yes	Capitalist class (2%)	New middle class (23%)
No	Old middle class (13%)	Working class (62%)

Source: Estimates compiled from (Wright 1997, 47) and (Zweig 2000, ch. 1).

Note: Although there is general agreement about the size of the capitalist class and the existence of a working-class majority, estimates of the exact percentages vary depending upon class definitions and methodologies.

such dreams are very limited. By the turn of the nineteenth century capitalist relations had predominated, and only 35 percent of the labor force was self-employed while 63 percent were wage/salary employees. By the 1980s the corresponding percentages would be 11 percent self-employed and 81 percent wage/salary employees (Reich 1986, 124).

The class structure in the United States has thus undergone significant change as a result of the changes associated with capitalist accumulation. The means of production, once widely held by independent commodity producers, have been concentrated in the hands of a small capitalist class. Today the richest 10 percent of USers owns 80 percent of stocks, bonds, and other business assets (Mishel et al. 2002, 279).

Radicals define the capitalist class as those who both own capital goods and control the wage labor of others (see Table 2.1). On this basis about 2 percent of the economically active population constitute this class. The working class on the other hand has grown from a relatively small class (5 percent in 1780) to the largest class in the United States (Reich 1986, 124).

The remaining 36 percent of USers are classified as middle class. Middle class usually implies a certain sort of lifestyle or certain level of income. Such a definition of middle class is very different from the one used within RPE. Radicals distinguish between the old and new middle classes. The old middle class includes those who own their own means of production but do not control on a regular basis the labor of others. They include small businesses (e.g., family stores and farms) as well as those who are self-employed, like plumbers or lawyers. Although they are their own bosses their fate is often determined by capitalist enterprises. Once a majority class in the United States, these independent commodity producers have shrunk to include only 13 percent of USers.

The new middle class consists of people who do not own their own means of production but do control the labor of others. They include managers and supervisors who usually work for a salary instead of a wage. While they control the labor of others, owners and top executives of the corporations also control them. The new middle class also includes managers who assist capitalists in realizing the largest possible surplus (sales, marketing), in keeping track of the surplus (accounting), and in investing surplus (finance). The salaries for those who make up the new middle class represent part of the surplus product shared by the capitalist.

Some radicals refer to the new middle class as the professional/managerial class and define it more broadly to include teachers, social workers, media professionals, and others whose major function is the reproduction of capitalist culture and class relations (see Ehrenreich and Ehrenreich 1979). Whatever the label and precise definition, this class hardly existed 200 years ago and is the product of capitalist accumulation and the growth of large-scale enterprises which it engenders.

The changes wrought by capitalism are not limited to the destruction of other economic systems, the creation of new class structures, and their concomitant social changes. The powerful forces of capital accumulation have also transformed capitalism itself. Although the system-defining features of capitalism have not changed, everything else has been the subject of continuous and dramatic change within the capitalist economy, for example, the kinds of products produced, technology used, location of production, and kinds of work done. The development of capitalism in the United States has produced a litany of such changes.

The changes brought on by capital accumulation have also included the institutional setting within which accumulation takes place. This context is a very important part of radical analysis and is called the social structure of accumulation (SSA). It includes the set of laws, institutions, and social customs and norms that structure and regulate domestic and international relations among capitalists, between capitalists and workers, among workers, and between government and the economy. The SSA concept is one of the ways that radicals explain how the economic system is interrelated with the rest of society.

Given the dynamic nature of profitmaking and the reinvestment of profits, the capitalist economy is constantly being transformed. The powerful dynamic forces emanating from the capitalist economy affect changes in social, political, and cultural areas. It is possible to identify three different social structures of accumulation representing distinct phases or stages in the development of U.S. capitalism. A particular complex of social, political, and cultural institutions defines each stage. Table 2.2 illustrates these stages and summarizes some of the important aspects of each SSA.

Each SSA tends to last for many years and is resistant to change because the social relationships on which it is based tend to be durable. On the other hand, the forces of change associated with the capital accumulation process are very great and tend to outgrow and undermine the favorable environment provided by the SSA. As the particular complex of institutions becomes less and less capable of creating a favorable accumulation environment, the rate of capital accumulation slows. When this happens, a period of decay sets in characterized by economic hard times, social disruption, and political conflict.

The Great Depression during the 1930s represents one such period of decay. The crisis in this view was not resolved until a new complex of social, political, and cultural institutions was created consistent with the needs of capital accumulation in this new stage of capitalist development. The construction of a new SSA is problematic according to radicals and depends upon the strength and actions of competing groups and classes, and political coalitions

Table 2.2

Structures of Accumulation, 1840–1970

Key SSA relations	Mid-19th century SSA (1840–1870s)*	Early-20th century SSA (1890–1920s)*	Mid-20th century SSA (1940–1960s)*
Capital-capital relations	Small businesses, local competitive markets	Large corporations (trusts), close financial-industry links, national monopolistic competition	Multinational corporations, dual economy, international monopoly competition, U.S. corporations dominant
Capital-labor relations	Labor process based on craft skill, extensive workplace control by skilled labor, strong craft unions in some industry	Technical control of labor, machine pacing, corporate welfare plans, unions weak and unrecognized	Labor accord, unions recognized with legal rights, collective bargaining, bureaucratic control of labor
Labor-labor relations	Craft-based distinctions between skilled and unskilled workers, open immigration	Homogenized labor, semiskilled labor becomes important	Segmented labor markets, unions strong among mass-production workers, racism and sexism
Government-economy relations	Limited government, free land at frontier, state aid for development of transportation, philosophy of individualism	State repression of unions, antitrust legislation, new state regulation of business, corporate liberal philosophy	Keynesian demand management, limited welfare state, regulation stabilization programs in agriculture, oil, and finance; state growth in education, R&D, and highways; Bretton Woods monetary system; U.S. military, political, and economic dominance in world; New Deal Democratic coalition

Source: Compiled from information in Kotz (1987).
Note: *The 1880s, 1930s, and the years since 1970 are periods of SSA decay and economic crises.

formed such as the New Deal Coalition in the 1930s. Many radicals argue that post–World War II SSA entered a long period of decay and restructuring from 1970 as result of globalization, the contradictions of which are to date still unresolved. This will be discussed in more detail in the section on theories of economic crises in chapter 5.

In the next three chapters we will show how the concepts and framework developed in this chapter are utilized in the theory of radical political economy.

Notes

1. Conventional economists frequently employ the metaphor of a small independent commodity-producing society to characterize the essence of capitalism.

2. In addition to moneylenders, profit (surplus) is shared with managers, merchants, and landowners. This raises the issue of productive and unproductive labor. In RPE unproductive labor is that which does not produce surplus product, but receives part of it. For the capitalist to realize profits, the surplus must be shared with those who help make it possible, such as managers who manage workers for the capitalist and merchants who market the product for the capitalist. For an extended discussion of this, see Resnick and Wolff (1987), 117ff.

References

Bowles, Samuel, and Richard Edwards. 1993. *Understanding Capitalism.* New York: HarperCollins.

Burawoy, Michael. 1982. *Manufacturing Consent.* Chicago: University of Chicago Press.

Ehrenreich, Barbara, and John Ehrenreich. 1979. "The Professional-Managerial Class." In *Between Labor and Capital,* ed. Pat Walker, 5–48. Boston: South End Press.

Hahnel, Robin. 1981. *Marxism and Socialist Theory.* Boston: South End Press.

Kotz, David. 1987. "Long Waves and Social Structures of Accumulation." *Review of Radical Political Economics* (Winter): 16–38.

Mishel, Lawrence, Jared Bernstein, and Heather Boushey. 2002. *The State of Working America 2002/2003.* Ithaca, NY: Cornell University Press.

Reich, Michael. 1986. "The Proletarianization of the Labor Force." In *The Capitalist System.* 3d ed., ed. Richard Edwards, Michael Reich, and Thomas Weisskopf, 122–131. Englewood Cliffs, NJ: Prentice-Hall.

Resnick, Stephen, and Richard D. Wolff. 1987. *Knowledge and Class.* Chicago: University of Chicago Press.

Roberts, Bruce, and Susan Feiner, eds. 1992. *Racial Economics.* Boston: Kluwer.

Wright, Erik Ohlin. 1997. *Class Counts: Comparative Studies in Class Analysis.*
    New York: Cambridge University Press.
Zweig, Michael. 2000. *The Working Class Majority: America's Best Kept Secret.*
    Ithaca, NY: Cornell University Press.

Further Reading

General

Baiman, Ron, Heather Boushey, and Dawn Sanders, eds. 2000. *Political Economy
    and Contemporary Capitalism.* Armonk, NY: M.E. Sharpe.
Best, Michael, and William E. Connolly. 1982. *The Politicized Economy.* 2d ed.
    Lexington, MA: D.C. Heath.
Bowles, Samuel, and Richard Edwards. 1993. *Understanding Capitalism.* New
    York: HarperCollins, chs. 1–7.
Edwards, Richard, Michael Reich, and Thomas Weisskopf, eds. 1986. *The Capi-
    talist System.* 3d ed. Englewood Cliffs, NJ: Prentice-Hall.
Lippit, Victor D., ed. 1996. *Radical Political Economy: Explorations in Alterna-
    tive Economic Analysis.* Armonk, NY: M.E. Sharpe.
Sherman, Howard. 1987. *Foundations of Radical Political Economy.* Armonk,
    NY: M.E. Sharpe.

Class

Barone, Chuck. 1998. "The Political Economy of Classism: Towards a More
    Integrated Multilevel View." *Review of Radical Political Economics* 30, no.
    2: 1–30.
Ehrenreich, Barbara, and John Ehrenreich. 1979. "The Professional-Managerial
    Class." In *Between Labor and Capital*, ed. Pat Walker, 5–48. Boston: South
    End Press.
Gibson-Graham, J.K, Stephen Resnick, and Richard Wolff, eds. 2001. *Re/pre-
    senting Class: Essays in Postmodern Marxism.* Durham, NC: Duke Univer-
    sity Press.
Resnick, Stephen, and Richard D. Wolff. 1987. *Knowledge and Class.* Chicago:
    University of Chicago Press, ch. 3.
Wright, Erik Ohlin. 1979. *Class Structure and Income Determination.* New York:
    Academic Press.
———. 1997. *Class Counts.* New York: Cambridge University Press.
Zweig, Michael. 2000. *The Working Class Majority: America's Best Kept Secret.*
    Ithaca, NY: Cornell University Press.

History

Beaud, Michael. 2001. *A History of Capitalism 1500–2000.* New ed. New York:
    Monthly Review Press.

Dobb, Maurice. 1963. *Studies in the Development of Capitalism.* New York: International Publishers.
Dowd, Douglas F. 1993. *U.S. Capitalism Development Since 1776.* Armonk, NY: M.E. Sharpe.
Zinn, Howard. 1995. *A People's History of the U.S.* Revised and updated ed. New York: Harper and Row.

Social Structure of Accumulation

Gordon, David M., Richard Edwards, and Michael Reich. 1982. *Segmented Work, Divided Workers: The Historical Transformation of Labor in the United States.* New York: Cambridge University Press.
Kotz, David. 1987. "Long Waves and Social Structures of Accumulation." *Review of Radical Political Economics* (Winter): 16–38.
Kotz, David, T. McDonough, and M. Reich. 1994. *Social Structures of Accumulation.* New York: Cambridge University Press.

3 THEORY OF PRODUCTION AND WORK

We can now begin applying the concepts and definitions developed in chapter 2, first by discussing the radical political economy theory of capitalist production, profits, and competition central to the radical understanding of the capitalist economy and its dynamics. This analysis is then extended to the radical theory of work, wages, and conflict in the capitalist workplace. These aspects of the capitalist economy are of course central to any economic theory, and the approach followed here is that of Bowles and Edwards (1993, chs. 8–11).

Capitalist Production

Profits

Radicals make a distinction between commercial profits and capitalist profits. Commercial profits are what is left over after selling something for more than it costs to purchase. "Buying cheap and selling dear" characterizes the profits of businesses engaged in buying and reselling products, such as retail and wholesale businesses. Commercial profits exist because of the failure of prices to equalize in all markets. You buy in one market at a lower price and sell the same commodity in another market at a higher price.

Capitalist profits, on the other hand, result from the labor process and the process of production. Although some radical economists analyze the rate of profit using a more traditional Marxist labor theory of value approach, the more simplified approach used here does not. Capitalist profit is the residual, the amount by which the output price exceeds the cost of producing the output. Profit is what is left over out of total revenue for the capitalist after materials used, wear and tear on machines, and labor employed have all been paid.

In the radical view, total profits include not only retained earnings and dividends, but rent and interest not usually included as profits. Total profits thus calculated are equal to the surplus product or value in capitalism. Capitalist profits are the driving force of capitalism, and RPE focuses on the rate and determination of such profits.

Rate of Profit

The rate of profit is defined as the amount of total profit divided by the value of capital goods owned.

$$r = \frac{R}{K}$$

where

r = profit rate
R = total profits
K = value of capital goods

The higher the rate of profit the more successful the capitalist. It measures the amount of profit made compared to the money invested. As we shall see, the rate of profit is the primary bellwether of the capitalist economy, and the fates of more than just capitalists are tied to the rate of profit.

It is possible for no surplus to exist, either due to the low productivity of the labor process or because society decides to designate any surplus as necessary consumption for all or some of the people. The question under capitalism is why does a surplus or profit exist?

The RPE answer to this question is much different from neoclassical economics, which claims that profits are essentially a return to capital, risk, or monopoly. In the neoclassical perspective profits are treated symmetrically as factor payments along with wages and other market-determined factor payments. However, profits are not determined by market exchange. Profit is a residual, what is left over after all market exchanges and payments have been made. Although you can call profit a factor payment to capitalists (as neoclassical economists do), strictly speaking it is not a factor payment in the same sense as wages or prices paid for raw materials that result from market exchanges (supply and demand).

If profits do not result from a market exchange, then where do they come from? The RPE answer to this question is complex. First the capitalists' claim to the surplus product is based not on voluntary exchange but on the unequal structural (class) position of capitalists and workers. Capitalists have a legal right to the means of production in the economy based on private ownership rights. This exclusive right—exclusive in the sense that only a very small percentage of the people (2 percent in the United States as shown in chapter 2) in a capitalist system are able to amass sufficient money capital to command the means of production—gives capitalists a monopoly of the productive property in the economy.

Second, private ownership of capital goods also gives to the capitalist a legal property right to the total output and thus total revenue of the firm. The residual that is left over after market payments to workers and replacement of the means of production used up is the surplus or profit produced by workers but claimed (legally) by capitalists. One can imagine firms without capitalists where the surplus produced belongs to the workers who decide democratically what to do with the surplus. Profits exist then and accrue to capitalists because of property ownership, just as the surplus product that accrued to feudal lords or slave owners derived from the unequal structural (class) position with serfs and slaves.

Although private ownership of the means of production is a necessary condition for capitalist profits, it is not sufficient for their long-run maintenance. The rate of profit depends upon the technology used in production, the fraction of total revenue needed to replace means of production used up, and control over the labor process. Radicals place great emphasis on control over the labor process as a determinant of the rate of profit. Private ownership of the means of production gives capitalists the legal right to control the labor process. However, the labor process is a contested terrain where the interests of workers and capitalists do not always coincide.

The resolution of this conflict affects the rate of profit. For example, the rate of profit, other things equal, will be higher the lower the level of wages and the harder workers work. Workers will, however, favor higher wages and a less-fatiguing, less-dangerous pace of work. The particular outcome is the result of class struggle and the outcome is often favorable to capitalists because of their power and control over the production process. However, capitalist domination is incomplete without some sort of additional mechanism to insure sufficient power over workers.

Historically there have been, broadly speaking, three different types of mediation regimes that have been used to try to resolve the conflict between workers and capitalists in ways that maintain capitalist domination: authoritarian, social democratic, and free market. Examples of authoritarian regimes include Nazi Germany, fascism in Italy under Mussolini, and dictatorships used in some Third World capitalist countries today. These are all political/military responses to class conflict that suspends political democracy, represses opposition political parties, and outlaws independent working-class organizations in favor of high profits and working conditions favorable to capitalists.

A very different mediation regime is social democracy, practiced in some European countries such as Sweden, Denmark, Norway, Austria, and Great Britain. Like authoritarian regimes, social democracy mediates the conflicting interests between workers and capitalists at the state level. However, in social democracy, national federations representing labor and capital bargain democratically over wages, working conditions, and the size of the capitalist surplus. The outcome of this social democratic process depends upon the relative political strength of different groups. In Sweden, where there is a great deal of labor solidarity and the labor movement is very strong, the results of national bargaining are usually very favorable to labor, while at the same time providing capitalists with sufficient profits and stability for capital accumulation. In Great Britain, where labor has not always been politically very strong, social democracy has been intermittent and capitalist interests have tended to predominate.

The third way that conflicting interests between capitalists and workers have been resolved is with a free labor market regime where control is based on the level of unemployment. The threat of unemployment is perhaps the most common way that workers' bargaining power with capitalists can be weakened, especially in the United States where unions are relatively weak and social welfare safety nets are inadequate. The right of exclusion and the right to hire and fire are legal property-based rights in capitalism. Any bargaining leverage workers have will be diminished in the face of unemployment, particularly when income support policies are inadequate as they are in the United States.[1]

Economic insecurity and the threat of economic insecurity place workers in a weak bargaining position, both in labor markets (lower wages) and inside the firm where workers are less able to resist speedup and dangerous or boring work situations. It is usually much more difficult for a worker to find another job than it is for a capitalist to find another worker. This asymmetrical relationship between capitalists and workers is for radicals one of the major factors ensuring high rates of profits, and low wages, and poor working conditions for workers.

Profits represent the surplus product in capitalism, and capitalists have a legal claim to this residual by virtue of their property rights. The power that comes from ownership of the capital goods gives the capitalist command over the labor process, including the right to hire and fire. It is the capitalist command over the productive labor process (and the particular regime of mediation) that is one of the major determinants of the rate of profit in RPE.

Determinants of the Rate of Profit

Although the rate of profit is a function of capitalist power, there are constraints other than working-class resistance. The actions of other capitalists, the rate of technological discoveries, availability of raw materials, and government policies all influence what individual capitalists are able to do. To understand these constraints it will be necessary to develop more fully the determinants of the rate of profit.

We can begin by expanding the simple rate of profit equation used above and analyzing its constituent parts more closely.

$$r = \frac{Y - W}{K}$$

where

r = profit rate
Y = value of net output
W = wages
K = value of capital goods owned

The value of the net output (Y) represents total sales revenue (S) minus the value of materials, tools, and equipment used up (M) so that $Y = S - M$. This can be expanded so that

$$Y = P_Z Z - P_M M \text{ where}$$

P_Z = price of output
Z = gross output
P_M = price of materials used and worn out equipment
M = amount of materials used and worn out equipment

The value of gross output (Z) is determined by the market price and the amount of output produced. There are in the radical view two determinants of the amount of output produced by workers, or what is more generally called labor productivity; the efficiency of labor (e) and the intensity of labor (d) so that

$Z = edL$

where

e = efficiency of labor in terms of output per unit of work done
d = intensity of labor in terms of work done per hour
L = total hours worked by labor force

Productivity is first of all determined by labor efficiency, the amount of output that can be produced for a given amount of work effort or intensity, that is, holding constant how fast and hard workers actually work. The major factors influencing labor efficiency are technology, quality of capital equipment, and the organization of the labor process or division of labor.

The second aspect of labor productivity is unique to RPE and highlights the variability of labor. Workers can work faster or more slowly, harder or more easily, producing correspondingly more or less output. The pace of work is called the intensity of labor. Output can be larger or smaller depending on how fast or hard workers can be compelled to work independently of the technology utilized by the capitalist. As we will see below, technology also can be used to increase the intensity of labor, not just labor efficiency.

The value of gross output then is determined by price of output (P_Z) multiplied by the amount of gross output (Z), which is a function of labor efficiency and labor intensity, that is, $Z = edL$. In order to arrive at the value of net output (Y) we need to subtract the costs of materials used and wear and tear on machines ($P_M M$). We are left with the value of net output. If we subtract wages (W) we are left with the amount of profits or surplus generated or

$R = P_Z Z - P_M M - W$

The rate of profit is determined comparing the profits generated to the value of capital goods owned or $r = R/K$. The value of capital goods is equal to the total capital goods owned (CG) multiplied by the price of capital goods (P_C). Profits are calculated on the total investment, which includes the firm's machinery, buildings, and other capital goods. However, it is rare for firms to actually utilize fully their capital stock, perhaps due to the level of demand. This idle capacity represents idle investment and does not actually generate any profits. Capacity utilization (cu) is thus an important determinant of the rate of profit. It will have a positive influence on the rate of profit, for example, a lower rate of capacity utilization due to a recession will yield a lower rate of profit and a higher rate of capacity utilization will bring results in a higher rate of profit.

The capacity utilization ratio (or the percentage of owned capital goods actually in use) is equal to the amount of capital goods in use (CG in use) divided by the total capital stock (CG) or $cu = \frac{CG\,in\,use}{CG}$. We can now factor all the determinants into the value of capital goods owned, the denominator of our rate of profit equation:

$$K = P_C \frac{1}{CU}\,CG\ in\ use$$

The reciprocal of the capacity utilization ratio is used because it has a positive relationship to the rate of profit.

Combining all our results we get an expanded equation:

$$r = \frac{P_Z Z - P_M M - W}{P_C \dfrac{1}{CU}\,CG\ in\ use}$$

where $Z = edL$. We are now prepared to analyze capitalist competition and the rate of profit.

Capitalist Competition

Competition and the Rate of Profit

Capitalists are driven by competition to get as much profit as possible. The rate of profit is the way they evaluate their success or failure. In RPE theory capitalists are more than just the marginal quantity adjusters and price takers in a neoclassical theory of perfect competition. To be successful capitalist firms must aggressively develop competitive strategies in order to achieve high rates of profit. These strategies can be analyzed in terms of the determinants of the rate of profit and their ultimate impact on the rate of profit.

In the competitive struggle for profits, capitalists must invest and devise strategies that improve the determinants of their rate of profit. Notice in Table 3.1 that some strategies to improve the determinants of the rate of profit can be contradictory. For example, while raising P_Z will improve profits it may cause capacity utilization (CU) to fall if sales decline, resulting in lower profits. Union busting may lower wages (improves profits) but workers might retaliate by working more slowly (lowers profits). Government policy to stimulate the economy and increase capacity utilization may also generate demands for higher wages that might lower profits. Capitalist strategies to improve profits are thus risky, making the future rate of profit difficult to predict.

Some of the determinants of the rate of profit are not easily changed. Workers will resist lower wages, and increasing labor intensity will be difficult unless workers can be compelled to work faster. Strategies to improve the efficiency of labor are limited by the current state of knowledge and technology.

Capitalists are constrained in other ways. Individual capitalists in their attempt to improve the determinants of their own rates of profits are brought into competition with other capitalists as they also try to improve their rates of profit. The actions and reactions of other capitalists limit what individual capitalists can do. A firm cannot always raise the price of its output (P_Z) or lower the prices they pay for materials or capital goods $(P_M$ and $P_C)$.

Dynamics of Competition

In the radical perspective capitalists are compelled to compete and strategize for higher profits. The competitive investment process is characterized by constant struggle as individual capitalists try

Table 3.1

Competitive Profit Strategies

Profit rate determinant	Capitalist strategy
1. Price of output (P_Z)	Gain market power so that prices can be raised.
2. Efficiency of labor (e)	Improve technology.
3. Intensity of labor (d)	Speed up the production line or hire more supervisors to control the pace of work.
4. Materials and machines used up (M)	Develop production methods that reduce amount of wasted materials or broken tools.
5. Price of materials and machines used up (P_M)	Find new supplier with lower prices.
6. Hourly wages (W)	Locate a source of cheaper labor or break up unions.
7. Price of capital goods used in production (P_C)	Find a cheaper supplier of the machines used in production.
8. Capital goods in use $(CG$ in use$)$	Develop production methods that use less equipment.
9. Capacity utilization ratio, or percentage of owned capital actually in use (CU)	Find markets for additional output, advertise, or lobby government to stimulate the economy, raising aggregate demand so that idle factories or machines can be put to use.

Source: Adapted from Bowles and Edwards (1993, 125).

to improve the determinants of the rate of profit in the face of competition. The focus here is on the dynamics of the capitalist competitive process rather than the more static equilibrium emphasis of neoclassical economic theory. Even if market clearing takes place, in the radical view the endogenous forces of capitalist profit strategizing produces dynamic forces that constantly change and alter the context of competition.

These endogenous competitive forces create continuous change. The dynamic process of reinvestment and capital accumulation is the central feature of the market process, not market clearing equilibrium, which in the radical view is not sustainable or central to capitalism. Competition is a struggle to alter what are treated as givens in neoclassical theory (technology, preferences, prices) and to change the nature of competition itself. Change is endogenous, not exogenous, in the RPE model of the firm.

The winners in capitalist competition are those who are more successful in devising strategies to circumvent the limits imposed by competition. These strategies can be divided into three categories: price competition strategies with given technology and market structures. Here firms are faced with a dilemma. If they raise prices then capacity utilization will fall, and if they lower prices capacity will be more fully utilized. The specific outcome in terms of the rate of profit is uncertain. In a price-competitive market profits are limited to a small markup over costs. Capitalists are continuously trying to find ways of lowering their price relative to their competitors. Such strategies include routine cost-cutting measures, for example, lowering wages, increasing labor intensity, or eliminating waste. Such strategies usually result in only small improvements in profits for successful firms.

Second, more dramatic improvement in profits comes from breakthrough strategies whatever the level of the average rate of profit. Developing a new product, discovering a new source of raw materials, developing a new process technology, or any other innovation allows a firm to break out of the limits of price competition. A breakthrough gives an advantage over its competitors, raising its rate of profit above normal. Such profits, sometimes referred to as superprofits by radicals, last only until rival firms catch up. However, the capitalist first with a breakthrough has the advantage of being first with subsequent breakthroughs. No firm whether it is ahead or behind can slacken its efforts to achieve breakthroughs.

Third, similar to breakthrough strategies are monopoly strategies that also yield significant improvements in the rate of profit. Here the goal of capitalists is to insulate themselves from competition. With monopoly power, firms can more easily change the determinants of the rate of profit without the retaliation of competitors. In RPE monopoly is a generic term used to refer to all forms of market concentration from single sellers (pure monopoly) to a few sellers (oligopoly).

Monopoly strategies are essentially designed to eliminate competition by (1) driving rivals out of business; (2) formal collusion and/or informal tacit agreements among rival firms not to compete; and (3) preventing new competitors from entering the market. Monopoly power strategies can be used with any of the determinants of the rate of profit, although power over P_z is the most important.

One example of a strategy to gain monopoly power is for a firm to set P_z lower than the costs of production, subsidizing losses with past superprofits or with the profits from other profitable subsidiaries in the corporation. The winners of such price wars are those capitalists with the most financial resources who can hold out the longest. Once rivals are eliminated or taken over, the victor raises prices and reaps a monopoly profit.

The Robber Baron Era at the turn of the nineteenth century in the United States epitomizes such strategies. Although moderated by antitrust legislation, public control is incomplete, leaving room for monopoly strategizing. Antitrust regulation is nonexistent internationally where much of contemporary strategizing takes place, for example, between Japanese, European, and U.S. capitalists.

Other monopoly power strategies include barriers to entry such as technical secrets, patents, exclusive marketing arrangements, and large initial start-up costs, as well as market-share strategies based on sales efforts. The horizontal dimension focus of RPE and the capitalist firm is on such monopoly power and breakthrough capitalist strategies. It is these profit strategies that in their view capture the essence of capitalist firms and capture the dynamic character of capitalism.

As a result, competition between firms, markets, and regions tends to produce unequal rather than equal rates of profits. While price competition and exit/entry of firms tend to establish a common average rate of profit for all firms, breakthroughs and monopoly power cause divergent profit rates. In the radical view, the forces that generate divergent profit rates tend to dominate, preventing a competitive equilibrium from being attained.

Economic Concentration

The neoclassical ideal of perfect competition is unattainable in capitalism, according to radicals. Capitalist competition creates ever-greater economic concentration, the degree to which the largest corporations control economic activity in an industry and in the whole economy. Greater size usually increases a corporation's ability to obtain higher profits. Larger size permits greater exploitation of decreasing costs, increases the firm's ability to achieve breakthroughs and monopoly power, and enhances the firm's political and bargaining power with respect to labor, finance, suppliers, and the government.

The evolution of U.S. corporations from small firms serving local markets to larger firms serving regional, national, and international markets gives evidence to this radical claim. Market concentration increased dramatically in the United States during the late 1800s and by 1904 oligopolists accounted for 32.9 percent of total manufacturing output. Although this percentage has since edged up slightly and half of all markets in U.S. manufacturing are concentrated, after 1970 market concentration declined due to dramatic increases in foreign competition (Scherer and Ross 1990, 82–85). Radicals predicted that the same forces (capitalist competition) that produced the domestic shakeout of corporations in the United States at the turn of the nineteenth century would produce a similar shakeout in world markets. The high level of domestic and international corporate merger waves in the 1980s and 1990s is evidence of this trend toward greater market concentration as corporations move to consolidate global markets (Du Boff and Herman 2001).

Although the degree of market power is an important aspect of capitalist competition, radicals are also interested in the control capitalists exercise over the whole economy (aggregate concentration). Gigantic multinational corporations dominate the economy. These corporations, like ExxonMobil, the largest U.S. corporation with $228 billion in year 2000 sales, have grown both in absolute size and control of aggregate economic activity, a persistence long-term trend in the United States since the early 1900s (Greer 1992, 202).

In the competitive drive for profits, some firms are driven out of business and others join together (often the result of hostile takeovers) in merges that are horizontal (firms in the same industry), vertical (firms producing different products but in the same stream of production, e.g., a steel company and an iron ore mine), and conglomerate (firms producing unrelated products). U.S. capitalism is now experiencing (1994–2001) its fifth wave of mergers distinguished by much higher acquisition values and a larger number of cross-border mergers. The ten largest mergers averaged $76 billion each, for example, America Online purchased Time Warner for $106 billion in year 2000 (Du Boff and Herman 2001). One of the largest multinational conglomerates is General Electric, which has hundreds of subsidiaries all over the world. Together with others these gigantic U.S. corporations control a disproportionate share of aggregate economic activity, making them truly corporate empires.

By 1971 the 100 largest manufacturing firms owned 49.3 percent of all corporate assets in manufacturing, more than the top 200 corporations held in 1948 (Greer 1992, 203; Heilbroner 1993, 118). Figure 3.1 shows the level of concentration for the top 500 and top 1000 industrial corporations. Notice that the addition of the second 500 largest industrial corporations to make up the top 1000 adds little to the total aggregate industrial concentration (5 percent more sales, 6 percent more profits, and 7 percent more jobs) compared to the much larger corporations in the top 500.

Figure 3.1 **Industrial Concentration**

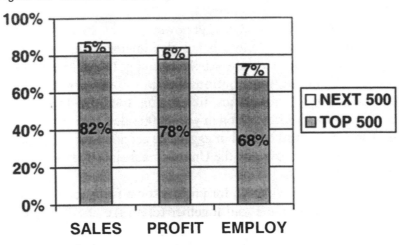

Source: Based on data from Edwards, Reich, and Weisskopf (1986, 73).

The high degree of economic concentration in the U.S. economy is, in the radical view, the product of capitalist competition for profits. Small-scale firms and competitive markets, although predominant in the early stages of capitalist development, are soon displaced by the very nature of the dynamic of capitalist competition. Competitive firms and relatively smaller firms still exist, but are part of a dual economy according to RPE. There were about 4.3 million incorporated businesses in 1994, and most of these make up the secondary sector that is in turn dominated by the very large firms with monopoly power in the primary sector. It is the concentrated primary-sector industries, such as steel, automobiles, transportation, telecommunications, banking and finance, and so on, that make up the commanding heights of the economy.

Production, profits, and competition are aspects of the economy that help to explain the nature of capitalism. The radical analysis brings together the three dimensions (command, competition, and change) to provide a unique understanding of capitalist firms. We move now to a discussion of the RPE analysis of the labor process within the firm with particular emphasis on work, wages, and conflict in the workplace.

Capitalism and the Labor Process

The Nature of Work

RPE is distinctive in its analysis of work and the labor process, two aspects of capitalism usually ignored in other perspectives. Neoclassical economics focuses on labor markets with little or no emphasis on the nature of work or the labor process. Labor markets are indeed an important aspect of capitalism, but equally if not more important in RPE is what happens to workers after they have agreed the sell their labor power in exchange for a wage or salary. Once they go to work and go through the factory or office doors, they enter the world of work, which is not in the radical view regulated by the laws of market exchange. In fact, under capitalism the world of work is regulated by command not voluntary exchange. Many U.S. constitutional rights held by citizens in the larger society, such as free speech and assembly, are not recognized within the factory or office where the rights of private property are sovereign.

At the most basic level, understanding the nature of work, radicals differ from others. In their view, people can enjoy not just the products of labor but can under the right conditions gain utility from the production process. Work is not necessarily something to be avoided, people can and do gain satisfaction from work. The view that work creates disutility or is unpleasant stems from the fact that many if not most kinds of work available to people in capitalism are unpleasant and alienating.[2] However, the disutility of work under capitalism does not in the radical view stem from the inherent nature of all work. Whether or not work is enjoyable depends upon the way work is organized, the ends toward which work is put, and who benefits. The same type of work can be enjoyable in one set of circumstances and quite unpleasant in another. For example, parenting is a challenging and demanding job, but it usually yields a great deal of satisfaction. The same kind of work in, say, day-care centers, where workers work for close to minimum wages under close supervision and have little say in how they do their job, yields little satisfaction. Under capitalism work is organized hierarchically in the service of capitalist profits.

Production and Conflict in Capitalism

We have already seen above in the discussion of the determinants of the rate of profit that workers' and capitalists' interests are frequently in conflict. This is because they occupy different positions in the production process. We can understand the basis for this conflict by considering unit labor costs, that is, the labor costs to the employer per unit of output. We can derive the unit labor costs from the rate of profit equation discussed above:

$$ulc = \frac{wage}{output} = \frac{w}{z} = \frac{w}{ed}$$

where

ulc = unit or average labor cost of producing each unit of output
w = wages per hour
z = output per hour
e = efficiency or amount of output per unit of work done
d = intensity or work done per hour

Profits will be higher the lower ulc or when w is lower, and when e and d are higher. When capitalists compete for profits they will adopt strategies that lower wages, increase the efficiency of labor, and increase the intensity of labor. Workers interests are frequently opposed to these strategies. Workers want higher wages to improve their standard of living, and less intense labor leaves workers less tired at the end of the day so that they may enjoy their leisure time more fully. Workers also benefit from fewer workplace accidents when the pace of work is slower.

Workers may or may not have an interest in higher efficiency (e), it depends upon the entire impact of new technology on other variables more directly related to workers' interests such as wages, employment, and labor intensity. When labor productivity is increasing it is usually easier to demand and get higher wages. However, such an outcome is dependent upon the relative bargaining strength of workers and capitalists. Often new technology is labor-saving and results in laid-off workers and/or greater capitalist control over the pace of work, allowing employers to increase labor intensity. So while improving efficiency may benefit workers, they are frequently placed in a position where it is possible for them to lose. This perhaps explains why workers often resist technological change.

It is the relative bargaining strength that determines the outcome of the contest between workers and capitalists. Wages for unionized workers are determined by collective bargaining and individually by nonunion workers. The state of the labor market (e.g., level of unemployment and degree of market concentration) establishes the range within which both capitalists and workers (or unions) can bargain. The specific wage level will also be limited by productivity and output prices. Within the range set by these factors, wages will be higher or lower depending upon the relative bargaining strength of workers and capitalists.

The Difference Between Labor Power and Labor

The intensity of labor, how much work is done per unit of time, is also determined by bargaining. The capitalist purchases labor power or the capacity to work in the market. The labor contract specifies that the worker will work for so many hours. However, the actual work done or labor is elastic and difficult to specify in advance.

This can be illustrated by comparing the purchase of labor power with the purchase of a machine. Capital equipment, unless it is defective, usually performs as specified when purchased. Capitalists do not have to extract performance from purchased machinery. The relation between purchased labor time and actual labor performed is much more problematic than this. In the radical view, the need to extract labor from labor power creates the need for elaborate management systems and techniques to get as much labor or work out of workers as possible. Workers of course resist and the labor process becomes a site of active struggle between capitalists and workers over the intensity of labor.

Workers are not guaranteed that when they work harder they will be paid more. Perhaps the best example given is the history of piece rates, where workers are paid so much for each piece they make. On the face of it, it would seem that the harder one works the higher one's wages will be. Unfortunately, the historical experience shows that once workers' proficiency develops to the point where they are earning above-average wages, employers cut piece rates. This experience has led workers to consciously withhold from employers knowledge of how fast they can work by "soldiering," working more slowly (Braverman 1974, chs. 4–5).

Control and the Capitalist Workplace

Capitalist firms are organized in ways that will maximize profits. Control over workers is an essential component of their competitive strategies. Capitalists and their managers and supervisors exercise power over workers ultimately because they have the legal right to hire and fire. Employers have the right to determine who will work and who will not work. Workers who resist or do not do what they are told can be fired. When there is high unemployment it is difficult for workers to find other jobs. In this case, the threat of being fired carries more weight, giving capitalists more effective control over workers. As we will see later in this chapter, in the radical perspective unemployment is seen as a permanent feature of U.S. capitalism giving employers power and control over workers.

Other capitalist strategies that deny workers access to jobs include lockouts and runaway shops. A lockout is when employers shut down production and lock workers out the workplace in an attempt to force workers to accept lower wages, a faster pace of work, or other working conditions unfavorable to workers. This strategy is effective when workers have few other employment alternatives and feel strong financial pressures. Such a strategy may cost capitalists very little if they have parallel plants producing the same products in other parts of the country or in other countries. Production in other parallel plants is merely stepped up to compensate for lost production in the locked-out plant.

Alternatively the capitalist may decide to permanently shut down a plant and move to new location. This is called a runaway shop and has been an effective strategy in the United States, where many plants have been shut down and moved to new locations in the southern states and in other countries like Mexico or Malaysia where workers are usually unorganized and more desperate, and thus willing to work for lower wages and under worse working conditions. Even the threat of a runaway shop can force concessions from workers, improving the rate of profit.

Capitalists also increase the power they have over employees through their social organization of the labor process. In order to get workers to produce as much profit as possible, capitalists organize the labor process hierarchically so that they can main tain control over workers and the labor process. A hierarchical organization is one where control is centralized with those at the top giving commands and those at the bottom complying with the decisions made by those in command. This feature of capitalism gives it a strong command economy basis and contrasts with the neoclassical emphasis on the voluntary exchange aspects of capitalism.

The social organization of the labor process in RPE is determined to a significant extent by capitalist strategies to control workers in order to extract as much work from them as they can. Employers devise various systems of control. Smaller firms use simple control or the drive system to lower unit labor costs by keeping wages close to the minimum. With little incentive to work hard, close supervision of workers is necessary to drive the workers. Simple control is based on the owner's or a hired manager's personal supervision.

Technical control is based on the use of technologies that give employers greater control over the pace of work. In this case machines control the pace of work, making supervisors less necessary. The assembly line is a good example of technical control.

Management controls the speed of the line, and workers are forced to keep up with the pace. However, if the speed of the assembly line is too great, workers may find ways to sabotage the line, bringing production to a halt. As in all systems of control, capitalists have to rely to some extent on workers' voluntary cooperation. Thus the speed of machinery is to some degree determined by bargaining power, and workers will have greater power when they are more organized.

Another system of control is bureaucratic control based on elaborate multilayered hierarchy, detailed work rules, job ladders, and seniority. A bureaucracy is a multilayered organization with an elaborate division of labor. Formal job descriptions exist for each job, detailing the duties and tasks to be done. Employees' performance is evaluated against their job descriptions.

In a bureaucracy jobs are organized hierarchically and are linked together with job ladders. Workers are hired for entry-level positions and then based on performance and seniority are promoted from within up the job ladder. In many cases, the skill differences between the rungs on the job ladder are insignificant. The primary purpose of job ladders is to motivate workers to comply with the rules/goals of the firm. Workers are given higher wages as they move up the job ladder. Although seniority guarantees greater wages and job security, it also makes those with seniority more compliant with company rules/goals. Such workers have a lot to lose if they are fired; and given corporate policies of hiring for entry-level positions, workers may have to accept a much lower paying entry-level job elsewhere.

The centralized power in bureaucracy is much more invisible than in other systems of control. Those who occupy positions of authority are merely enforcing "company policy" and what appear to be "objective" job descriptions. Owners and their chief executive officers have the real power to determine the rules, and they make all the decisions concerning competitive profit strategies. Capitalists are shielded from direct confrontation with workers, and the onus of control rests with capitalist underlings, the middle-level managers. These members of the new middle class are in positions that often place them in direct confrontation with the working class.

Bureaucratic control apparently does not obviate the need for supervisors to direct workers, evaluate performance, promote, fire, and hire. U.S. capitalism has the most elaborate system of bureaucratic control with the highest ratio of supervisors to production workers of any other capitalist country (Thurow 1985, 145). As the competitive struggle between capitalists intensifies on a world scale, U.S. corporations with more "bureaucratic fat" are finding themselves at a competitive disadvantage. This has resulted in a significant degree of corporate downsizing in the United States in the recent years. Downsizing has not, however, been at the expense of maintaining control over workers and their intensity of work as capitalists have found other means to control their workforces.[3]

Although simple, technical, and bureaucratic systems of control currently coexist in the United States (sometimes even within the same firm), these systems have evolved historically at different times in capitalism development. Simple control was the first system developed in the early stages of capitalism. Technical control came around the turn of the nineteenth century, followed by bureaucratic systems of control during and after World War II (Edwards 1979). In response to the rapid globalization and accelerating global competition in recent years, new corporate forms of control are evolving that maintain strong centralized control over strategic decision making while decentralizing other aspects of the enterprise (Harrison 1984).

Technology and the Labor Process

Technical control was addressed briefly above. The radical analysis of technology and capitalism goes much further than this. Technological change affects the rate of profit in many ways. It may reduce the amount of materials used or the wear and tear on machinery (M). It may also reduce the amount of capital goods in use (CG in use). All of these effects will increase the rate of profit.

Technological change may also lower unit labor costs (ulc) by increasing labor efficiency (e), increasing labor intensity (d), or lowering wages (w).

In the radical view, technology is a social product only partially determined by scientific principles. Although such laws and engineering principles limit the range of alternatives available to capitalists, there is considerable latitude. Capitalists will invent and choose technologies that enhance their rate of profit. In some instances this may mean adopting technology that is less efficient (lower e) but gives the capitalist greater control over workers. Such control allows the capitalist to extract more work out of workers, an increase in labor intensity (d). As long as the decline in labor efficiency is more than offset by the increase in labor intensity, ulc will fall and the rate of profit will be higher.

Thus competitive capitalist profit strategies do not necessarily result in greater efficiency in the radical view. This difference comes from the way they define efficiency as greater output per hour of work holding constant the intensity of labor. The radical definition of efficiency allows for greater understanding of command and conflict in capitalism as well as the economy's contradictory nature. Adopting technologies that are less efficient and increase the pace of work is a rather perverse result from a social point of view, even though from the capitalists' perspective it may increase their rates of profit. According to radicals, capitalists rarely if ever adopt technologies that increase workers' control over the labor process or enhance worker autonomy.

Technological change is the source of much conflict given the way the labor process is organized in capitalism. By increasing efficiency, technology can raise profits without lowering wages or increasing labor intensity, but workers will naturally want to share in the gains of efficiency and may ask for higher wages. Driven by competitive forces inherent in capitalism, capitalists will resist worker demands for higher wages. Workers may respond by sabotaging production (decreasing e), or "working to rule" or otherwise slowing down the pace of work (lower d). In the radical view, workers must constantly struggle in order to have their needs met, but capitalists have the upper hand because of their legal property rights that gives them the right to hire and fire. In the radical view, technology should be a liberating force freeing people from material scarcity and from the need to work as hard or as much.

Technical change has also produced machine pacing of work. Managers are able to increase the rate of profit by increasing the intensity of labor. Such a strategy is called speedup and is a frequent source of conflict between workers and managers. Another result of technical change is deskilling, the simplification of tasks so that workers with fewer skills can be hired to do them. Skilled workers can get higher wages because they are difficult to replace and on the job they have more control over the labor process because of their knowledge. By using production methods that require less skilled labor and more unskilled labor, capitalists can increase their rates of profit by lowering wages and raising labor intensity.

Again workers have every reason to resist such methods of production. Lower wages, less autonomy and control over their own work, greater labor intensity, and greater alienation do not contribute to workers' well-being or human development. Historically deskilling has played an important role in capitalist development. Early in the development of capitalism most productive methods required highly skilled workers who were part of particular crafts. The practice of their craft required a great deal of scientific knowledge about technology and production processes.

Capitalists had very limited power over these craft workers because of their knowledge and control over production. To overcome this, U.S. capitalists at the end of the nineteenth century designed new productive methods (called "scientific" management) that deskilled jobs by separating conception from execution. The planning, drafting, and engineering aspects of jobs were taken away from workers and placed in new departments under the control of management. This accounts in part for the growth of the new middle class, people who specialized in these new positions. With the conception of a task removed from the shop floor, all that remained for workers was the basic execution of simple tasks as if working for a distant brain. A great stigma was attached to these workers who "only" worked with their hands.

Deskilling and wresting control from workers caused a pro-tracted struggle and this period of time (1880–1920) represents a very bitter period in U.S. labor history. Today deskilling efforts have permeated the majority of workplaces and has left few jobs untouched, including the many white-collar occupations created by the early deskilling strategies. Radicals estimate that many if not most jobs require little skill and are repetitive and boring. It is ironic that those doing these jobs today carry the stigma of "working with their hands." The stultifying effect of such work and the constraints it places on human development is the focus of much of the contemporary radical analysis of alienation.

Unions and Collective Bargaining

Given the structural basis for the conflicting interests of workers and capitalists highlighted by RPE, individual workers stand little chance of success when challenging their capitalist employers. The only way workers can achieve some bargaining power is through unity and solidarity with each other rather than each worker trying to make a separate deal with his or her employer.

Unions are formal labor organizations that try to accomplish this. They collectively bargain on behalf of members. Unions negotiate contracts that include wage rates, fringe benefits, and employment practices, which include work standards and rules, job assignments, worker health and safety, and grievance proce-dures. Union contracts help to protect workers from the uncon-strained command of the capitalist.

Union success depends upon a number of variables such as the degree of labor unity and solidarity, state of the labor market, skill of union officials, labor laws, and the strategies adopted by capitalists. In the United States the labor movement has been responsible for improvements over the twentieth century in wages, benefits, and working conditions. The labor movement is responsible for the passage of legislation regulating sweatshops, child labor, minimum wages, and occupational health and safety.

Despite these gains the labor movement has been less successful and more violent than in many other countries. Radicals attribute this to the difficulties of organizing an ethnically and racially diverse, geographically separated workforce and the much more aggressive actions of U.S. capitalists when compared to their Western European counterparts. The use of government-imposed injunctions, the military, and private security forces, such as Pinkerton's in coal mining, are examples of the capitalist strategies used against striking workers (Fantasia 1988, ch. 2).

Hundreds of U.S. workers were killed and wounded in this war between labor and capital. Until the Wagner Act established the legal right for workers to form unions in the 1930s, few workers belonged to unions. Although many workers now belong to unions (15 percent of the labor force), the percentage is significantly smaller than most other capitalist countries (e.g., Sweden 80 percent, United Kingdom 44 percent, and Germany 35 percent). (Gardner 1988, 461) The U.S. percentage has been declining since the mid-1950s, a trend that has accelerated since 1980 as bargaining power has shifted away from workers to capitalists who have intensified their union-busting efforts to raise profits at workers' expense. Some corporate strategies, such as those used in the 1989 United Mine Workers strike against the Pittston Coal Company in West Virginia, are reminiscent of the more aggressive (and violent) actions of capitalists sixty years ago.[4]

Although radicals are very pro-union, they are critical of the corruption and the lack of union responsiveness to the needs of rank-and-file members that exist in a few unions. However, corruption and lack of responsiveness plague other organizations including corporations, yet rarely are these organizations criticized as harshly as unions are. Despite the shortcomings of unions they are the only institution in the United States that represents workers' interests. Radicals support rank-and-file attempts to end corruption and to democratize their unions.

Discrimination

One capitalist strategy that has been a powerful tool in preventing unionization and keeping workers divided is discrimination.

In the radical perspective it can be profitable for capitalists to discriminate and to exploit ethnic/racial and gender divisions within the workforce. Capitalists benefit by having an easily exploitable group that can be hired for very low wages. Racism and sexism promote or perpetuate the belief that women and people of color are of less value and can therefore be paid less and worked harder than their white male counterparts.

Capitalists also profit in another way. Discrimination can be used as a divide-and-conquer strategy by pitting workers against each other. The use of black strikebreakers and tactics that fuel racial antagonism within a factory are powerful strategies that have been used in the United States to prevent unionization and keep workers divided. The exploitation of these divisions within the workforce means that the wages of all workers are lower than they would be if male and female and black and white workers were united. Discrimination in the radical view then harms all workers and benefits primarily capitalists (Reich 1981).

In the neoclassical view discrimination is costly to capitalists, because they cannot hire workers on the basis of individual productivity. In this mainstream view, the capitalist market system provides incentives not to discriminate and it is believed that over time such incentives will lead to the elimination of discrimination. In the radical perspectives markets tend to perpetuate discrimination in the long run. Although some loss in efficiency may result from discrimination (negative effect on profit), dividing workers against each other also results in less bargaining power for all workers that results in lower wages and greater intensity of labor (positive effect on profit). Radicals argue that the net effect will be higher profits, giving capitalists powerful financial incentives to discriminate. In this view, the competitive struggle for profits will force the nondiscriminating capitalists to discriminate along with the discriminating capitalist, as long as it is profitable to do so. Thus, in the radical view, capitalism promotes discrimination and provides a fertile environment for discriminatory attitudes.

Unemployment and Control

Ultimately the most reliable factor keeping unit labor costs low is unemployment. In RPE labor markets do not clear like other markets. The typical situation is one of excess workers and thus unemployment. This means that the supply curve of labor is horizontal over the relevant range. For the labor market to clear means that the quantity of labor time demanded by firms equals the quantity of labor time supplied by workers at the prevailing wage. Everyone who wants a job at the prevailing wage has one and there is no involuntary unemployment.

Full employment implies that everyone who has a job could easily get another one at a similar market-clearing wage. Although this situation is possible in capitalism, in the RPE perspective it is unlikely to persist because it conflicts with high rates of profit. If workers can find other comparable jobs quickly and easily, then they are more likely to resist speedup, work-rule changes, unsafe working conditions, or other capitalist initiatives. This could have negative effects on the rate of profit and would induce capitalists to lay off workers.

The resulting unemployment reestablishes the threat of being fired and allows capitalists to implement strategies that restore the rate of profit at workers' expense. Unemployment acts as a safety valve that maintains high rates of capitalist profits and is a more or less permanent feature of U.S. capitalism. (Alternatives to unemployment as a way of regulating class conflict in capitalism were discussed earlier in this chapter.)

With the RPE theory of production and work in a capitalist economy complete, the next chapter explores the way radicals extend their analysis of the capitalist economy to a capitalist system. For a capitalist economy to work it must be joined with other institutions in society. RPE provides a way of understanding how the capitalist organization of production and the labor process is joined with the rest of society, making up a capitalist system that extends beyond just the economic system.

Notes

1. For the current state of unemployment compensation in the United States, see Marc Baldwin, "Beyond Boom and Bust: Financing Unemployment Insurance in a Changing Economy," *National Employment Law Project Report 2000*, available at: http://nelp.org/ui/boomandbust.htm; and Harry Holzer "Unemployment Insurance and Welfare Recipients: What Happens When the Recession Comes?" The Urban Institute, December 2000.

2. There is a well-developed literature from an RPE perspective analyzing the debilitating aspects of work, or alienation, under capitalism. See citations under the "Worker Alienation Under Capitalism" heading in the further reading section at the end of this chapter.

3. Surveys done in 2001 by Families and Work Institute (www.families andwork.org/) show that workers are feeling increasingly overworked and overwhelmed. See also Juliet Shor *The Overworked American* in the further reading section.

4. For an extended analysis of the decline of U.S. unions, see Michael Goldfield, *The Decline of Organized Labor* and Rick Fantasia, *Cultures of Solidarity,* chs. 2 and 6; see George DeMartino for a very insightful analysis in "U.S. Labor Faces an Identity Crisis"—all in the further reading section. On the Pittston strike, see Moe Seager, "One Day Longer Than Pittston," *Zeta Magazine,* October 1989, pp. 13–24.

References

Bowles, Samuel, and Richard Edwards. 1993. *Understanding Capitalism.* New York: Harper and Row.

Braverman, Harry. [1974] 1998. *Labor and Monopoly Capital: The Degradation of Work in the Twentieth Century.* 25th anniv. ed. New York: Monthly Review Press.

Du Boff, Richard, and Edward Herman. 2001. "Mergers, Concentration, and the Erosion of Democracy." *Monthly Review* (May):14–29.

Edwards, Richard C. 1979. *Contested Terrain: The Transformation of the Workplace in the Twentieth Century.* New York: Basic Books.

Edwards, Richard C., Michael Reich, and Thomas Weisskopf, eds. 1986. *The Capitalist System.* 3d ed. Englewood Cliffs, NJ: Prentice-Hall.

Fantasia, Rick. 1988. *Cultures of Solidarity: Consciousness, Action, and Contemporary American Workers.* Berkeley: University of California Press.

Gardner, H. Stephen. 1988. *Comparative Economic Systems.* New York: Dryden Press.

Greer, Douglas F. 1992. *Industrial Organization and Public Policy.* 3d ed. New York: Macmillan.

Harrison, Ben. 1984. *Lean and Mean.* New York: Basic Books.

Heilbroner, Robert. 1993. *The Making of Economic Society.* 9th ed. Englewood Cliffs, NJ: Prentice-Hall.

Reich, Michael. 1981. *Racial Inequality.* Princeton, NJ: Princeton University Press.

Scherer, F.M., and David Ross. 1990. *Industrial Market Structure and Economic Performance.* 3d ed. Boston: Houghton Mifflin.

Thurow, Lester. 1985. *The Zero-Sum Solution: Building a World-Class American Economy.* New York: Simon and Schuster.

Further Reading

Profits and Capital Accumulation

Bowles, Samuel, and Richard Edwards. 1993. *Understanding Capitalism.* New York: HarperCollins, chs. 8–9.

DuBoff, Richard B. 1989. *Accumulation and Power: An Economic History of the United States.* Armonk, NY: M.E. Sharpe.

Edwards, Richard, et al. 1986. *The Capitalist System.* 3d ed. Englewood Cliffs, NJ: Prentice-Hall, ch. 3.

Green, Francis, and Robert Sutcliffe. 1987. *The Profit System.* Middlesex, England: Penguin Books.

Resnick, Stephen A., and Richard D. Wolff. 1987. *Knowledge and Class.* Chicago: University of Chicago Press, ch. 4.

Weeks, John. 1981. *Capital and Exploitation.* Princeton, NJ: Princeton University Press.

Labor Process, Working Class Struggles, and Unions

Bowles, Samuel, and Richard Edwards. 1993. *Understanding Capitalism.* New York: HarperCollins, chs. 10–11.

Boyer, Richard O., and Herbert M. Morais. 1955. *Labor's Untold Story.* New York: United Electrical, Radio, and Machine Workers of America.

Brecher, Jeremy. 1997. *Strike!* Rev ed. Boston: South End Press.

DeMartino, George. 2000. "U.S. Labor Faces an Identity Crisis." In *Political Economy of Contemporary Capitalism,* ed. Ron Baiman, Heather Boushey, and Joanne Saunders, 130–136. Armonk, NY: M.E. Sharpe.

Edwards, Richard et al., eds. 1986. *The Capitalist System.* 3d ed. Englewood Cliffs, NJ: Prentice-Hall, ch. 4.

Fantasia, Rick. 1988. *Cultures of Solidarity: Consciousness, Action, and Contemporary American Workers.* Berkeley: University of California Press.

Franklin, Stephen. 2001. *Three Strikes: Labor's Heartland Losses and What They Mean for Working Americans.* New York: Guilford Press.

Freeman, Richard B., and James L. Medoff. 1984. *What Do Unions Do?* New York: Basic Books.

Goldfield, Michael. 1987. *The Decline of Organized Labor in the United States.* Chicago: University of Chicago Press.

Hinshaw, John, and Paul Le Blanc, eds. 2000. *U.S. Labor in the 20th Century: Studies in Working Class Struggles and Insurgency.* Amherst, NY: Humanity Books.

Moody, Kim. 1997. *Workers in a Lean World: Unions in the International Economy.* New York: Verso.

Nissen, Bruce, ed. 1999. *Which Direction for Organized Labor?* Detroit: Wayne State University Press.

Wharton, Amy S. 2002. *Working in America: Continuity, Conflict, & Change.* 2d ed. New York: McGraw Hill.

Wood, Ellen Meiksins, Peter Meiksins, and Michael Yates, eds. 1998. *Rising From the Ashes? Labor in the Age of "Global" Capitalism.* New York: Monthly Review Press.

Wright, Erik Olin. 1997. *Class Counts: Comparative Studies in Class Analysis.* New York: Cambridge University Press.

Yates, Michael D. 1998. *Why Unions Matter.* New York: Monthly Review Press.

———.2000. "The 'New Economy' and the Labor Movement." *Monthly Review* (April): 28–42

———. 2003. *Naming the System: Inequality and Work in the Global Economy.* New York: Monthly Review Press.

Zweig, Michael. 2001. *The Working Class Majority: America's Best Kept Secret.* Ithaca, NY: Cornell University Press.

Worker Alienation Under Capitalism

Braverman, Harry. [1974] 1998. *Labor and Monopoly Capital: The Degradation of Work in the Twentieth Century.* 25th anniv. ed. New York: Monthly Review Press.

Cooley, Mike. 1980. *Architect or Bee? The Human/Technology Relationship.* Boston: South End Press.

Edwards, Richard C. 1979. *Contested Terrain: The Transformation of the Workplace in the Twentieth Century.* New York: Basic Books.

Fraser, Jill Andresky. 2001. *White-Collar Sweatshop: The Deterioration of Work and It's Rewards in Corporate America.* New York: Norton.

Garson, Barbara. 1988. *The Electronic Sweatshop: How Computers Are Transforming the Office of the Future into the Factory of the Past.* New York: Simon and Schuster.

Gordon, David M., Richard Edwards, and Michael Reich. 1982. *Segmented Work, Divided Workers: The Historical Transformation of Labor in the United States.* New York: Cambridge University Press.

Haight, Alan Day. 2001. "Burnout, Chronic Fatigue, and Prozac in the Professions: The Iron Law of Salaries." *Review of Radical Political Economics* 33: 189–202.

Hamper, Ben. 1991. *Rivethead: Tales from the Assembly Line.* New York: Warner Books.

Hudson, Ken. 2001. "The Disposable Worker." *Monthly Review* (April): 43–55.

Rayman, Paula. 2001. *Beyond the Bottom Line: The Search for Dignity at Work.* New York: St. Martin's Press.

Schor, Juliet. [1991] 1993. *The Overworked American: The Unexpected Decline of Leisure.* Reprint ed. New York: Basic Books.

Sheppard, Harold L., and Heal Q. Herrick. 1972. *Where Have All The Robots Gone? Worker Dissatisfaction in the 1970s.* New York: Macmillan.

Tilly, Chris, and Charles Tilly. 1998. *Work Under Capitalism.* Boulder, CO: Westview Press.

Discrimination

Albelda, Randy, Robert Drago, and Steven Shulman. 2001. *Unlevel Playing Fields.* Cambridge, MA: Economic Affairs Bureau.

Berneria, Lourdes. 1979. "Reproduction, Production and the Sexual Division of Labour." *Cambridge Journal of Economics* 3: 203.

Cherry, Robert. 1989. *Discrimination: Its Economic Impact on Blacks, Women, and Jews.* Lexington, MA: D.C. Heath.

Edwards, Richard C. et al., eds. 1986. *The Capitalist System.* 3d ed. Englewood Cliffs, NJ: Prentice-Hall, chs. 7–8.

Fusfeld, Daniel R., and Timothy Bates. 1984. *The Political Economy of the Urban Ghetto.* Carbondale: Southern Illinois University Press.

Green, Charles. 2001. *Manufacturing Powerlessness in the Black Diaspora.* New York: Altamira Press.

Hartman, Heidi. 1976. "Capitalism, Patriarchy, and Job Segregation by Sex." *Signs* (Spring): 1

Folbre, Nancy. 1994. *Who Pays for the Kids? Gender and the Structures of Constraint.* New York: Routledge.

Lieman, Melvin. 1993. *The Political Economy of Racism: A History.* London: Pluto Press.

Mutari, Ellen. 2000. "Feminist Political Economy." In *Political Economy and Contemporary Capitalism,* ed. Ron Baiman, Heather Boushey, and Joanne Saunders, 29–35. Armonk, NY: M.E. Sharpe.

Mutari, Ellen, Heather Boushey, and William Fraher. 1997. *Gender and Political Economy: Incorporating Diversity into Theory and Policy.* Armonk, NY: M.E. Sharpe.

Reich, Michael. 1981. *Racial Inequality.* Princeton, NJ: Princeton University Press.

Roediger, David. 1991. *The Wages of Whiteness.* New York: Verso.

Sen, Gita. 1980. "The Sexual Division of Labor and the Working-Class Family: Towards a Conceptual Synthesis of Class Relations and the Subordination of Women." *Review of Radical Political Economics* 12, no. 2: 83.

Sherman, Howard. 1987. *Foundations of Radical Political Economy.* Armonk, NY: M.E. Sharpe, ch. 5.

Shulman, Steve, and William Darity, Jr., eds. 1989. *The Question of Discrimination: Racial Inequality in the U.S. Labor Market.* Middletown, CT: Wesleyan University Press.

"Special Issue: The Political Economy of Race and Class." 1985. *Review of Radical Political Economics* 17, no. 3 (Fall).

"Special Issue: Feminist Political Economy." 2001. *Review of Radical Political Economics* 33, no. 4 (Fall).

4 THE CAPITALIST SYSTEM

The RPE analysis of the capitalist organization of the labor process, profits, and competition is incomplete without an understanding of the critical role that the rest of society plays in capitalism. In the radical view a capitalist economy could not exist without a supporting set of "noneconomic" institutions or culture. A capitalist economy requires a capitalist society or system to function and reproduce itself over time. Capitalist power and domination of the labor process extends into these other spheres. Although the radical analysis in these areas is quite extensive, we will limit our discussion to the RPE theory of the state and two aspects of culture: ideology and patriarchy.

Cultural Domination

Ideology and Reproduction

Capitalist domination over workers would be incomplete if capitalists did not also dominate culture and use existing cultural creations to their advantage. For example, most workers accept the right of capitalists to own the places of work and to exercise their property rights, even though workers may be unhappy with the outcome of capitalist decisions. Workers may struggle and bargain for different outcomes, but for the most part they do not struggle against the right of capitalists to own capital and control the labor process. If workers did not accept these parameters or rules of the game, then workers might try to change the organization of production. Such efforts would impede the capitalists' ability to control the labor process and interfere with profit making.

To maintain its position and privileges, the capitalist class must ensure the continuation of capitalist organization: markets, property rights, and control over labor. The social process that ensures this maintenance and continuation is called reproduction, a process in all societies that promotes continuity from one generation to the next.

Capitalist relations of production are based on domination and exploitation, according to radicals. This creates a legitimation problem; how can workers be convinced to accept an economic system based on domination and exploitation? An economic system can be legitimated as long as ideology, the dominant ideas and values in society, justifies the way the economy is organized.

In RPE, the formation of ideology is a process characterized by struggles among groups with competing interests. Under capitalism, the capitalist class, because of its dominant economic position and great financial wealth, is able to influence the idea-formation process in ways that ensure that the dominant ideology will be procapitalist.

Education

One institution that plays a key role in the formation of ideology is education. Why is it that students in the United States are not taught to be critical of the economic system? The radical answer to this question is that corporations and businesses are able to influence schools in direct (school board members, trustees) and indirect (school financing, research grants) ways. Furthermore, few educators are willing to risk antagonizing the business community, which controls the economic fate of so many. This affects both the content of education (what is taught) as well as its organization.

Another way that schools legitimate capitalism in the RPE perspective is by certification. If children enter schools as undifferentiated individuals (an assumption), they leave school ranked, ordered, and certified to fill positions in the capitalist-generated economic order. Those who do well in school are certified to hold the better-paying positions in the corporate hierarchy and those who do not do well will get the low-paying positions (assuming there are enough jobs to go around).

In the radical view, schooling perpetuates the illusion that everyone has the same chance to succeed and that those who do well are inherently superior to those who do not do well in school. Capitalist hierarchy is thus legitimated as a meritocracy, a system where it is believed that positions are allocated on the basis of free competition and individual merit.

Of course, capitalist ownership is excluded from this "merit" system. Many ownership positions are transferred to others through inheritance independent of merit considerations. Even the wealth accumulated by noninheritors seems to be more a function of luck than merit (Thurow 1975). In the case of non-property-based positions, radicals argue that schooling outcomes are not the result of free and open competition. First, the quality of schooling varies across schools districts. Schools in economically poor districts such as those in inner cities or poor working-class areas are able to spend much less per pupil than school districts located in wealthier neighborhoods. The result in the United States is what has been referred to as "savage inequalities" in educational outcomes (Kozol 1992). Of course, higher income families can afford to send their children to expensive private schools and thereby avoid public education altogether.

Second, children from different classes accumulate different forms of cultural capital. Cultural capital is a set of accumulated psychological and intellectual abilities. Such abilities are necessary to participate in particular cultures and subcultures. In capitalist societies, the very different life experiences of different classes produce distinct subcultures with corresponding forms of cultural capital. When education is structured on the basis of capitalist and middle-class forms of cultural capital, working-class children are at a disadvantage making it difficult to compete effectively. Ironically when working-class children fail they are blamed for being either stupid or culturally inferior or both (Macleod 1995, chs. 2, 8; Steinitz and Solomon 1986, chs. 1, 7).

The cultural biases of education are reinforced with tracking systems that label and channel children very early into college preparatory, general education, business, and vocational tracks. Such tracking contributes further to the class stratification of schools that tends to mirror the class structure of capitalism (Bowles 1986).

The lack of money to make ends meet, frequent unemployment, and physically exhaustive work make it difficult for working-class families to provide the same family environment that other families with higher incomes and economic security are able to provide for their children. The economic stresses and strains of working-class life mean that working-class children often do not have a home environment conducive to intellectual growth and development. As a result much talent fails to be developed within the working class

A final argument from the RPE perspective on education is that there is a hidden curriculum, one whose purpose is to prepare children to fill their proper roles in capitalist society. In this view, the hidden curriculum is more important than the open curriculum that emphasizes cognitive skills. Working-class children are taught to do as they are told, to accept authority and boredom, and to work for external rewards (grades) in preparation for working-class jobs. Children from other classes, particularly those who go on to college, will be given more freedom and choice reflecting the relative autonomy required by the jobs they will fill in the capitalist-generated hierarchy. The hidden curriculum also reinforces unequal gender roles (patriarchy) and racial inequality (white racism), which reproduce the divisions among workers important to capitalist divide and conquer profit strategies discussed earlier in chapter 3.

These factors account for the fact that the best predictor of an individual's economic success is his or her parents' economic position. Children from working-class families tend to become the next generation of workers. The same holds true for children of other classes, so that the before and after school distribution of people across classes remains largely unchanged. Therefore, radicals argue that schooling merely reproduces and legitimates existing class positions (Bowles 1986; Ryan 1981, 16ff).

Media

According to radicals, the free flow of ideas under capitalism is free as long as it does not challenge capitalist domination of the labor process. In the United States, capitalists have direct control of the media. They own the major network radio and television stations, newspapers, and other print media. Corporate sponsorship and advertising also mean that television and radio programming as well as the print media are dependent upon corporate funding. Increasingly this is true even for "public" radio and television in the United States. This makes it difficult to get funding for programming or print media that air views and publish articles that are hostile toward or critical of capitalism. Business interests are thus able to exert control over the major channels of communication and this imparts a procapitalist mass media bias according to radicals (Herman and Chomsky 2002).

One example of such bias is the dramatic decline since 1980 in the number of "labor desks" at major newspapers and the consequent lack of media coverage of labor issues. The Soviet Union's coal miners' strike in 1989 got far more media coverage than one of the most bitter coal miners' strikes in Pittston, West Virginia (Seager 1981). The U.S. mass media has a long history of distorting labor news and perpetuating negative images of both workers and unions. From newspapers to the evening news, from television sitcoms to Hollywood movies, labor and unions are painted with a negative brush. It is no wonder so many people have such negative views of labor and unions (Puette 1992). The mass media and telecommunications industries are no exception to the capitalist tendency toward greater centralization and concentration (Bagdikian 1997). In the past twenty years mergers have created a media monopoly dominated by such media giants as Time Warner that control the flow information and determine the nature of entertainment.

Capitalist domination of the media, together with education, ensures that the dominant ideology propagated in society will legitimate capitalist domination of production and the labor process. In these ways, the capitalist class is able to ensure that its position of economic privilege and domination is maintained and reproduced over time.

Patriarchy

There are other aspects of the capitalist system that help to reproduce capitalist relations from one generation to the next. Capitalists are able to use culture in other ways to enhance their economic power and control. Racism and sexism, although predating the development of capitalism, have been modified in ways that not only perpetuate discrimination but enhance capitalist exploitation, as was shown in chapter 3. Racism and sexism have both received considerable research attention by radicals. However, our discussion here will be limited to sexism as an example of the kind of analysis done from this perspective.

Male domination extends into all spheres in society, including the family, government, economy, and culture. This system of male domination in society is called patriarchy. Patriarchy is a complex system or set of relationships that maintains and perpetuates male dominance in society. When capitalism came into existence, patriarchy had already been entrenched for many centuries. Radical analysis (usually referred to as socialist feminism) focuses on the interrelationships between these two systems of domination, one based on class domination and the other based on gender domination.

Capitalism has modified the patriarchal system in significant ways. For example, in the United States, prior to the development of capitalism, the family was the basic productive unit and the home was the site of most production. The removal of production from the home to the capitalist factory has transformed family functions. With production removed from the home, family functions were reduced to procreation and nurturing. With the development of wage labor, it was possible for women to become financially independent from men and thus liberated from male domination. However, this was not to be, as women's access to jobs was restricted and their pay held to levels much lower than men. Unable to achieve financial independence, most women had to depend upon men and marriage for their economic well-being, reinforcing patriarchy.

In the late nineteenth century, a new ideology emerged called the domestic code. These ideas and beliefs glorified and justified women's new and restricted role as family homemakers and caretakers, subservient to their husbands' wishes and commands. This new restricted role was viewed as the natural and inevitable outgrowth of women's unique feminine nature. Of course, many women— especially black women—worked as wage laborers outside the home and inside other people's homes as maids and nannies. They worked to supplement their husbands' meager wages, and many women worked because they chose not to marry (even though it often meant economic deprivation) or because they were widowed. For the workingwoman who was single, either by choice or circumstance, poverty was the rule. Today's "discovery" of the feminization of poverty is thus nothing new; women have always been disproportionately poor.

In the late 1800s protective legislation, promoted by the domestic ideology, was passed. This legislation legally defined jobs according to their supposed suitability for men and women. Women were thus legally kept out of certain jobs thought to be dangerous or unsuitable to a woman's "delicate nature and sensibility." Women's jobs outside the home became extensions of their work inside the home—maids, seamstresses, waitresses, and so forth. Of course, forcing women into new domestic roles and denying women equal access to training and education also insured that women would be unable to compete with men for the better or higher paying jobs.

While all this had the effect of reinforcing patriarchy, it also benefited capitalism. First, it provided capitalists with a group of workers who could be paid less than men for doing the same work, thus increasing profits. Second, keeping men and women separate made it more difficult to achieve working-class unity, further benefiting employers. Third, placing all the family responsibility on men made them more willing to work hard and endure exploitation in the name of sacrificing for their families. Finally, with wives at home to soothe and nurture their husbands after a hard day's work, men could be exploited more intensively by their employers. Related to this is that although most men are dominated in the workplace, men have been able to dominate at home, to be "kings of their own castles." This, it is argued, has made men more willing to submit to capitalist domination in the workplace.

In these ways, capitalism has taken patriarchy and bent it to serve capitalist interests. It has done so in a way that has also reinforced male dominance and patriarchy. Today patriarchy and economic discrimination are under attack by many women and their male allies. A majority of women work outside the home and some have made economic gains. However, despite such progress, both patriarchy and discrimination are still firmly entrenched at the beginning of the twenty-first century. The feminization of poverty, continued crowding of most women in low-paying traditional female jobs, the fact that women still receive only 70 cents for every dollar a man gets, but still do most of the domestic work and child care are cited by radicals as evidence of continuing discrimination (Albelda, Drago, and Shulman 2001). Many radicals believe that because capitalism and patriarchy reinforce each other, gender equality is limited by capitalist organization of workplaces.

Capitalism and the State

In the RPE perspective, the state or government plays an important supporting role, without which capitalism could not function. Unlike the minimalist state advocated by Adam Smith and by many later neoclassical economists, radicals do not idealize the role of government in capitalism. They argue that extensive state intervention in economic affairs is necessary in capitalism and supported by capitalists as long as it affects the rate of profit and the accumulation of capital positively, and assists in reproducing capitalist relations of production over time.

The form of state and nature of government intervention vary across capitalist systems and depend upon the particular mediation regime in force: authoritarian, social democracy, or free market. The following discussion, drawn in part from Bowles and Edwards (1993), is limited primarily to the United States and the free labor market regime (see their ch. 17).

Economic Role

The government, as producer, distributor, microeconomic regulator, and macroeconomic manager, plays an important economic role. Government affects how the economy works by altering market relations (horizontal), relations between capitalists and workers (vertical), and the rate and direction of economic growth (change). In the RPE perspective, the survival and workability of capitalism requires a constantly growing government role in response to the dramatic technical and social changes brought about by the endless capitalist search for profits. The dynamics of capitalism have provoked demands for more government involvement by many, including corporations, workers, unions, and consumers. Radicals argue that such growth in government has not been in opposition to capitalism but because of capitalism.

Government establishes the rules of markets and private property. Such rules are not always self-evident and are usually subject to varying interpretations. Different groups and classes have different ideas concerning what the rules should be, how existing rules should be interpreted, and how the rules should be enforced. When it comes to trying to change the rules, more often than not it is business interests that dominate.

The restriction of property rights so that textile mills in the 1800s could divert the flow of rivers and streams without the permission of existing landowners along rivers benefited mill owners in the United States (Bowles and Edwards 1993, 415). The lack of property rights to air as well as water have allowed factories to pollute both with impunity. The inability to control pollution today in spite of widespread citizen support to do more, and in spite of the passage of U.S. environmental legislation in the 1970s, is testimony to capitalist control of government.

Radicals cite rules such as tariffs and other forms of regulation that protect businesses from competitive market forces. Regulatory agencies and legislation, although ostensibly created to protect the public interest, have often been used to protect industries from competition and enforce cartel-like market sharing. In response to growing economic concentration and the growth of large corporate empires, antitrust legislation was passed in the United States around the turn of the twentieth century. Although generally viewed as a response to growing citizen pressure to regulate large-scale industry and prevent monopoly, capitalists saw it as a way of regulating competition that effectively enforced cartel-like arrangements that were difficult to enforce otherwise. The accelerated growth of government intervention in the United States into economic affairs on behalf of business interests has created what radicals call the corporate liberal state.

On the other hand, labor in the United States has also been able to affect the rules of the game, but not without long and hard struggles. These efforts have been prompted by the need to protect themselves from the power of gigantic corporations and the probusiness, corporate liberal state. The Wagner Act of 1935 gave workers the right to collectively bargain in unions rather than compete against each other in labor markets. The right to form unions and collective bargaining came much earlier in most other capitalist democracies.

Workers' rights to collective bargaining were later seriously restricted in the United States by the Taft-Hartley Act in 1947. Legislated on behalf of corporate employers, this act restricted significantly the ability of workers to organize and establish unions responsive to workers' needs. For example, the act prohibited sympathy strikes by workers in unrelated industries, making classwide action difficult (Fantasia 1988, 55–59). This accounts in part for the fragmentation of unions and the labor movement in the United States.

The Occupational Safety and Health Act, successfully legislated in 1970 after more than fifty years of trying by labor, protects the health and safety of workers on the job. However, this success was qualified by business lobbying which insured underfunding and later lack of enforcement by often probusiness and antilabor presidents. So, while labor is able to influence the rules, their success comes only after years of hard struggle and is usually qualified significantly by business counterefforts to make such legislation less effective than it otherwise would be in protecting labor's interests.

The steady drive for profits and accumulation in capitalism has led to the international expansion of capital. With the commanding heights of the economy in the hands of U.S. multinational corporations, the support for tariffs has declined while support has grown for protecting U.S. corporate investments and markets abroad. Such protection required an extensive and expensive worldwide military system and involvement in wars to protect corporate interests abroad.

Although radicals recognize that all societies need to defend themselves, they argue that the real threat to the United States since World War II has been considerably less than our present defense system would indicate. Capitalist domination of ideology, discussed above, produced an anticommunist ideology that governed U.S. foreign policy from 1948 to 1991 and rationalized the growth of the defense establishment as necessary to the defense of "freedom and democracy" and the defeat of "communism and totalitarianism." This ideology was used effectively in garnering the necessary public support for a large military establishment and worldwide military presence. Since the 1989 breakup of the Soviet Union and the fall of communism in Eastern European countries, citizen attempts to reduce the size of the U.S. military have been met with new claims of a perceived military threat by rogue nations and international terrorism. However, the real purpose of such a large defense establishment has been, in the radical view, to protect U.S. corporate interests abroad and to boost corporate profits at home with lucrative defense contracts.

Other tendencies within capitalism have likewise required extensive growth in government economic involvement. Economic instability has created the need for government stabilization policies and macroeconomic management of the economy. Defense expenditures have made it possible to keep domestic levels of aggregate demand high, keeping capitalists' profits high at home as well as protecting their interests abroad.

In the RPE perspective, military Keynesianism has been the preferred solution to economic stagnation by U.S. corporations. Military spending generates high rates of profit and does not interfere with capitalist domination of the labor process in the way other forms of spending (welfare) might by increasing the social wage, thus raising the floor below which wages cannot be driven. Military spending is also much easier to sell to the public, because people's fears can more easily be exploited. Of course, it has the added bonus of protecting capitalist foreign markets and investment abroad.

However, military spending is a mixed blessing for capitalists. First, while it has perhaps moderated business cycles, in the radical perspective cyclical downturns are necessary in U.S. capitalism for the maintenance of high rates of profit. (Business cycles will be analyzed in the next chapter.) If military spending prevents this mechanism from working, capitalists may resort to raising prices (inflation) in order to maintain high rates of profit. Second, high rates of excess capacity in U.S. factories during the 1980s, when military spending was at a peak, provides evidence that military spending has limited ability to overcome stagnation. Finally, while government spending on the military may benefit the military industry, capitalists in other industries may be hurt by the diversion of resources (engineers and other skilled labor, research and development resources, etc.).

Of course, even without these problems, radicals believe that the high levels of military spending in the United States since World War II have been largely unjustified and extremely wasteful. However, significant reductions in defense spending will not be forthcoming, in the radical view, as long as U.S. corporations have substantial foreign investments and stakes in foreign markets, particularly in the Third World, and are able to dominate government decision making. And for now, U.S. foreign policy is being ruled by a fear of rogue nations and international terrorism, which have conveniently replaced the old fear of the Soviet Union. Such foreign "enemies" have the added feature of deflecting public attention from serious domestic problems and class conflict.

The failure of capitalist markets to generate sufficient employment or guarantee livable wages has created demands by citizens for government income support policies such as minimum wages, welfare, unemployment compensation, and Social Security. Although the United States has one of the smallest welfare states of any other advanced capitalist country and the lowest income support levels (and highest rate of poverty), income support policies make a real difference to millions of USers even though such policies are extremely inadequate. Income support policies also tend to legitimate capitalism (part of the reproduction process) by tempering somewhat, particularly in the minds of those not in need of income support, some of the most glaring failures of capitalism.

The growing failure of capitalist markets to equate private and social costs (negative externalities) has led to citizen demands for public safety legislation, such as environmental, consumer product safety, and occupational health and safety legislation. The need for such legislation is especially great in the advanced stages of capitalist development and the advent of large-scale industry and mass production, which generates a proliferation of such externalities.

Although some of the externalities experienced within capitalism are evident in other systems, capitalism has its own distinctive process of generating and dealing with such problems. For example, an often-cited cause of negative externalities is that our system is not capitalist enough. If private property were extended to air and water (amenity rights) then pollution would become a violation of individual property rights, a form of trespass. While this sounds like a capitalist solution, capitalists would be the first ones to oppose it. The demands by citizens in the United States for public safety legislation have consistently been met with business opposition. With the election of a procorporate administration in 2000, the capitalist assault on environment has been strengthened considerably. As long as capitalists can avoid the effects of these externalities (e.g., avoid congestion, foul air, dirty water) their preferred solution seems to be to do nothing. To the extent that they favor doing anything, they favor solutions that impose the greatest financial burden on other classes.[1]

In the radical view then, government plays a vital economic role in capitalism. While the capitalist state can be a threat to business interests when it acts on behalf of citizen demands, capitalists are usually strong enough to prevent such demands from being fully met. On the other hand, much of government intervention is on behalf of capitalists. The corporate liberal state or what some radicals call "corporate collectivism" characterizes the capitalist state.

Class Conflict and the State

What government can do is limited, in the radical view, by capitalism, because of the effects government can have on the rate of profit. This generates considerable conflict over public policies, particularly economic policy. In RPE, a major underlying source of political conflict is generated by the class structure of capitalism and the divergent interests it generates.

In the radical view, capitalists are able to dominate the policymaking process in several different ways, even when the capitalist economy is joined together with a political democracy such as in the United States. The capitalist class has great financial wealth, giving it a disproportionate ability to finance political campaigns, pay for lobbying, and offer inducements to politicians and policymakers regardless of party affiliation. According to radicals, the financial levers and political party bosses in both parties are controlled by the corporate wealthy in the United States Radicals often refer to both the Republican and Democratic parties as the "Money Party," representing the moneyed interests of society (Brouwer 1998).

As discussed above, members of the business class also tend to dominate ideology, the idea making process, through ownership of the mass media and corporate advertising. In addition, their control of major foundations and think tanks—such as the Ford Foundation, Rockefeller Foundation, Brookings Institution, American Enterprise Institute, Committee for Economic Development, and Foreign Policy Association—gives them a great deal of influence over major policy initiatives that flow from these elite planning institutions.

Finally, if these direct and indirect means of domination are insufficient, capitalists have a trump card. In a democracy where there is one-person one-vote, what is to stop the working-class majority from voting in prolabor candidates or a social democratic government with policies that threaten corporate interests? According to radicals, the one-person one-vote system of democratic rule in the United States has becomes a one-class one-veto system (Bowles and Edwards 1993, 430ff).

Suppose that the citizens of a particular city, state, or nation elect a government that passes legislation that guarantees full employment, provides adequate social welfare for all, and protects the natural environment. This is financed in part by higher taxes on the corporate wealthy, transferring part of the economic surplus to government that normally would go to capitalist profits. Full employment would also have adverse effects on the rate of profit because of the diminished threat of being fired.

Corporations might respond with a capital strike or capital flight until the "business climate" improves. Businesses can do this by withholding investment or transferring their operations to another city, state, or nation. In either case, slower economic growth leads to more unemployment and lower incomes. The government's popularity will decline and, given capitalist domination of the media, government will be blamed and it is likely that a new government will be elected that is more willing to meet business needs and improve the "business climate."

Government policies that might improve the rate of profit are summarized in Table 4.1. Like capitalist profit strategies, a government's policies to improve corporate profits can be contradictory. For example, government contractionary policies to maintain unemployment may reduce capacity utilization as well as depress hourly wages and raise labor intensity.

Although a general labor strike is always possible to force consideration of labor interests, the history of capitalism in the United States is replete with examples of the use of court injunctions, federal troops, and local police against labor and other groups in support of capitalist class interests. (For the history of the U.S. labor movement see end of chapter for further reading). Current labor law (Taft-Hartley Act) in the United States prohibits even sympathy strikes by workers in unrelated industries, for example, steel workers in support of a coal miners' strike. Labor has been stronger in countries like Sweden or Norway and they have been more successful in advancing working-class interests. However, the degree of working-class unity/solidarity and the degree of capitalist-class benevolence/cooperation necessary for such success is lacking in most capitalist countries.

Radicals argue, therefore, that there are limits to democratic decision making in a capitalist system. The capitalist class has the means and methods to ensure that any contest over political power and the direction of government policy is settled in favor of capitalists' economic interests. In some countries where political democracy has historically threatened these interests, democracy has been suspended. Examples include Chile, South Korea, Brazil, Iran, Guatemala, and El Salvador.

Even though there is a strong historical association between capitalism and political democracy, in the radical perspective capitalism is consistent with many different political forms, including fascism and dictatorships. Furthermore, in countries where political democracy has taken root, the extension of the political

Table 4.1

Government Policies and the Rate of Profit

Profit rate determinant	Government policies to raise profits
Hourly wage (W)	Maintain enough unemployment to depress wages; resist pressures to increase minimum wage.
Prices of output (P_z)	Use military and political power to obtain adequate foreign markets for output.
Output per unit of work done (e)	Subsidize research in applied science; promote job training.
Amount of work done (d)	Fail to enforce occupational safety and health standards or reduce standards.
Amount of materials and depreciation (M)	Support research in improved technology.
Price of materials and capital goods (P_M)	Allow businesses bigger depreciation allow ances on capital equipment; use U.S. power to gain access to cheap raw material such as oil.
Capital goods in use (CG in use)	Repeal regulations requiring waste-treatment equipment.
Capacity utilization ratio (CU)	Maintain growing and predictable level of demand for goods through macroeconomic policies.
Price of capital goods (P_C)	Grant tax credits for investment; allow accelerated depreciation.
Profits tax rate	Reduce corporate tax rate.

Source: Adapted from Bowles and Edwards (1993, 425).

franchise from property owners to the working class had to be fought for by working people, women, and minorities such as people of African heritage. Even with the franchise, when such groups threaten the interests of the owning classes, political democracy can be suspended.

This does not mean that the owning class is viewed as monolithic in RPE—it is not. It does mean that the cards are stacked in favor of capitalists, and that it is always an uphill struggle for workers and other citizen groups to gain enough leverage to get even minimal legislative relief from the adverse effects of capitalism. Capitalists have control over the major levers that control the economy. Without their cooperation, no government can stay in power for very long.

The picture we have painted of the capitalist system is incomplete. However, important parameters of the system have been traced out. In the RPE perspective, government and culture, traditionally either left out of economic analysis or their roles minimized, play an extensive and vital role in maintaining and perpetuating the capitalist economy. Capitalist organization of the economy requires supporting and complementary "noneconomic" institutions or social structures of accumulation. These supporting roles are assured, according to radicals, because capitalist domination of production and the labor process enables this class to dominate other institutions and culture in society.

Notes

1. For a more complete radical analysis of capitalism and environmental concerns, see John Bellamy Foster, *Marx's Ecology: Materialism and Nature* (New York: Monthly Review Press, 2000); Martin O'Conner, ed., *Is Capitalism Sustainable? Political Economy and the Politics of Ecology* (New York: Guilford Press, 1994). See also *Capitalism, Nature, and Socialism: A Journal of Socialist Ecology.*

References

Albelda, Randy, Robert Drago, and Steve Shulman. 2001. *Unlevel Playing Fields.* Cambridge, MA: Economic Affairs Bureau.

Bagdikian, Ben Haig. 1997. *The Media Monopoly*, 5th ed. Boston: Beacon Press.

Bowles, Samuel. 1986. "Schooling and Inequality." In *The Capitalist System*, 3d ed., ed. Richard Edwards, Michael Reich, and Thomas Weisskopf, 235–247. Englewood Cliffs, NJ: Prentice-Hall.

Bowles, Samuel, and Richard Edwards. 1993. *Understanding Capitalism.* New York: Harper and Row.

Brouwer, Steve. 1998. *Sharing the Pie: A Citizens Guide to Wealth and Poverty in America.* New York: Henry Holt.

Fantasia, Rick. 1988. *Cultures of Solidarity.* Berkeley: University of California Press.

Hermon, Edward S., and Noam Chomsky. 2002. *Manufacturing Consent: The Political Economy of the Mass Media.* New York: Pantheon.

Kozol, Jonathan. 1992. *Savage Inequalities: Children in America's Schools.* New York: Harper Perennial.

Macleod, Jay. 1995. *Ain't No Makin' It: Leveled Aspirations in a Low-Income Neighborhood.* Rev. ed. Boulder, CO: Westview Press.

Puette, William. 1992. *Through Jaundiced Eyes: How the Media View Organized Labor.* Ithaca, NY: ILR Press.

Ryan, William. 1981. *Equality.* New York: Pantheon.

Seager, Moe. 1989. "One Day Longer Than Pittston." *Zeta Magazine* (October): 13–24.

Steinitz, Victoria Anne, and Ellen Rachel Solomon. 1986. *Starting Out: Class and Community in the Lives of Working-Class Youth.* Philadelphia: Temple University Press.

Thurow, Lester. 1975. *Generating Inequality: Mechanisms of Distribution in the U.S. Economy.* New York: Basic Books.

Further Reading

Ideology and Legitimation

Berger, Peter L., and Thomas Luckmann. 1967. *Social Construction of Reality.* Garden City, NY: Anchor Books.

Fine, Ben. 1981. *Economic Theory and Ideology.* New York: Holmes and Meier, ch. 1.

Wisman, Jon. 1979. "Legitimation, Ideology-Critique, and Economics." *Social Research* 46, no. 2 (Summer): 291–320.

Education

Alexander, Karl L. et al. 1987. "School Performance, Status Relations, and the Structure of Sentiment: Bringing the Teacher Back In." *American Sociological Review* 2 (October): 665–682.

Apple, Michael. 1988. *Teachers and Texts: A Political Economy of Class and Gender Relations in Education.* Reprint ed. Boston: Routledge.

———. 1995. *Education and Power.* 2d ed. New York: Routledge.

Aronowitz, Stanley, and Henry A. Giroux. 1993. *Education Still Under Siege: The Conservative, Liberal, and Radical Debate Over Schooling.* 2d ed. South Hadley, MA: Bergin and Garvey.

Bernstein, Basil. 1979. *Class, Codes and Control,* vol. 3. Boston: Routledge.

Bourdieu, Pierre, and Jean-Claude Passeron. 1990. *Reproduction in Education, Society, and Culture.* 2d ed. Beverly Hills, CA: Sage.

Bowles, Samuel, and Herbert Gintis. 1976. *Schooling in Capitalist America.* New York: Basic Books.

Freire, Paulo. 1993. *Pedagogy of the Oppressed.* New York: Continuum.

Giroux, Henry A. 2001. *Theory and Resistance in Education.* South Hadley, MA: Bergin and Garvey.

Kneller, George F. 1984. *Movements of Thought in Modern Education.* New York: John Wiley, ch. 6.

Kozol, Jonathan. 1992. *Savage Inequalities: Children in America's Schools.* New York: Harper Perennial.

Macleod, Jay. 1995. *Ain't No Makin' It: Leveled Aspirations in a Low-Income Neighborhood.* Rev. ed. Boulder, CO: Westview Press.

Rosenfeld, Gerry. 1993. *Shut Those Thick Lips: A Study of Slum School Failure.* New York: Waveland Press.

Steinitz, Victoria Anne, and Ellen Rachel Solomon. 1986. *Starting Out: Class and Community in the Lives of Working-Class Youth.* Philadelphia: Temple University Press.

Weiler, Kathleen. 1988. *Women Teach for Change: Gender, Class, & Power.* South Hadley, MA: Bergin and Garvey.

Willis, Paul. 1977. *Learning to Labor: How Working Class Kids Get Working Class Jobs.* New York: Columbia University Press.

Media

Bagdikian, Ben Haig. 1997. *Media Monopoly.* 5th ed. Boston: Beacon Press.

Herman, Edward. 1996. "The Propaganda Model Revisited." *Monthly Review* (July–August): 115–128.

Herman, Edward S., and Noam Chomsky. 2002. *Manufacturing Consent: The Political Economy of the Mass Media.* New York: Pantheon.

MacDougall, A. Kent. 1988. "Boring Within the Bourgeois Press," Parts One and Two. *Monthly Review* (November–December).

Mantsios, Gregory. 2002 "Media Magic: Making Class Invisible." In *Race, Class, and Gender in the U.S.* 5th ed., ed. Paula Rothenberg, 563–571. New York: Worth Publishing.

Mazzocco, Dennis. 1994. *Corporate Television's Threat to Democracy.* Boston: South End Press.

McChesney, Robert. 2000. *Rich Media, Poor Democracy.* New York: New Press.

Parenti, Michael. 1993. *Inventing Reality: The Politics & the Mass Media.* 2d ed. New York: St. Martin's Press.

Puette, William J. 1992. *Through Jaundiced Eyes: How the Media View Organized Labor.* Ithaca, NY: ILR Press.

Rowse, Arthur E. 2001. *Drive By Journalism: The Assault on Your Need to Know.* Monroe, ME: Common Courage Press.

State

Block, Fred. 1987. *Revising State Theory.* Philadelphia: Temple University Press.

Bowles, Samuel, and Richard Edwards. 1993. *Understanding Capitalism.* New York: HarperCollins, ch. 13.

Bowles, Samuel, and Herbert Gintis. 1986. *Capitalism and Democracy.* New York: Basic Books.

Brouwer, Steve. 1998. *Sharing the Pie: A Citizens Guide to Wealth and Power in America.* New York: Henry Holt.

Carnoy, Martin. 1984. *The State and Political Theory.* Princeton, NJ: Princeton University Press.

DeGrasse, Robert W. 1983. *Military Expansion, Economic Decline.* Armonk, NY: M.E. Sharpe.

Domhoff, G. William. 2001. *Who Rules American: Power and Politics.* New York: McGraw-Hill.

Edwards, Richard C. et al., eds. 1986. *The Capitalist System.* 3d ed. Englewood Cliffs, NJ: Prentice-Hall, ch. 5.

Ferguson, Thomas. 1989. "By Invitation Only: Party Competition and Industrial Structure in the 1988 Election." *Socialist Review* 4: 73–103.

Harrington, Michael. 1978. "Corporate Collectivism: A System of Social Injustice." In *Ethics, Free Enterprise, and Public Policy,* ed. Richard T. De George and Joseph A. Pichler, 43–56. New York: Oxford University Press.

Parenti, Michael. 1974. *Democracy for the Few.* New York: St. Martin's Press.

Riddell, Tom. 1988. "The Political Economy of Military Spending." In *The Imperiled Economy Book II: Through the Safety Net,* ed. Robert Cherry et al., 227–238. Riverside, CA: Union for Radical Political Economics.

Sherman, Howard J. 1987. *Foundations of Radical Political Economy.* Armonk, NY: M.E. Sharpe, ch. 8.

Patriarchy and White Racism

Amott, Teresa, and Julie A. Matthaei. 1996. *Race, Gender, & Work: A Multicultural Economic History of Women in the U.S.* Rev. ed. Boston: South End Press.

Barera, Mario. 1979. *Race and Class in the Southwest.* Notre Dame, IN: Notre Dame University Press.

Brenner, Johanna. 1998. "On Gender and Class in U.S. Labor History." *Monthly Review* (November).

———. 2001. *Women and the Politics of Class.* New York: Monthly Review Press.

Holmstrom, Nancy. 2002. *The Socialist Feminist Project: A Contemporary Reader in Theory and Politics.* New York: Monthly Review Press.

Jagger, Alison. 1988. *Feminist Politics and Human Nature.* Totowa, NJ: Rowman and Littlefield, chs. 6,8, and 10.

Jones, Jacqueline. 1985. *Labor of Love, Labor of Sorrow: Black Women, Work, and the Family from Slavery to the Present.* New York: Basic Books.

Kessler-Harris, Alice. 1982. *Out to Work: A History of Wage-Earning Women in the United States.* New York: Oxford University Press.

———. 2001. *In Pursuit of Equity.* New York: Oxford University Press.

Lerner, Gerda. 1986. *The Creation of Patriarchy.* New York: Oxford University Press.

Marable, Manning. 2000. *How Capitalism Underdeveloped Black America.* Updated ed. Boston: South End Press.

Matthaei, Juliet. 1992. "Marxist-Feminist Contributions to Radical Economics." In *Radical Economics*, ed. Bruce Roberts and Susan Feiner, 117–144. Boston: Kluwer Academic.

Mutari, Ellen, ed. 1997. *Gender and Political Economy: Incorporating Diversity into Theory and Policy.* Armonk, NY: M.E. Sharpe.

Sargent, Lydia, ed. 1981. *Women and Revolution.* Boston: South End Press.

"Special Issue: Feminist Political Economy." 2001. *Review of Radical Political Economics* 33, no. 4 (Fall).

"Special Issue: The Political Economy of Race and Class." 1985. *Review of Radical Political Economics* 17, no. 3 (Fall).

Takaki, Ronald. 1993. *A Different Mirror: A History of Multicultural America.* Boston: Little, Brown.

Zaretsky, Eli. 1986. *Capitalism, the Family, and Personal Life.* Rev. and exp. ed. New York: Harper and Row.

5 DYNAMICS OF CAPITALISM

The focus of this chapter is on the RPE critical analysis of the dynamics of the capitalist economy. Our discussion will be limited to three of the most important of these capitalist tendencies: poverty and inequality, imperialism, and economic crises. These contradictions, along with others, are seen as serious enough faults in capitalism for radicals to question the long-run viability and desirability of capitalism.

Capitalism and Inequality

Although the extent of inequality varies widely across capitalist countries (among advanced industrial capitalist countries it is greatest in the United States), inequality in the distribution of income and wealth found in capitalist societies is in the radical perspective inherent in the capitalist mode of production and the exploitation of labor. The necessity of substantial income inequality offsets in large measure the great productive capacity of capitalism.

Wealth distribution data reveal a tremendous disparity of wealth holdings. A very small percentage of people in the United States own more property than the combined assets of the overwhelming majority of people (see Figure 5.1). In 1998 the richest 10 percent owned 70.9 percent of all wealth, leaving only 29.1 percent of the wealth for the remaining 90 percent of USers. In fact, the richest 1 percent owned 38.1 percent and the richest 5 percent owned 59.4

Figure 5.1   **Distribution of Household Wealth, 1998**

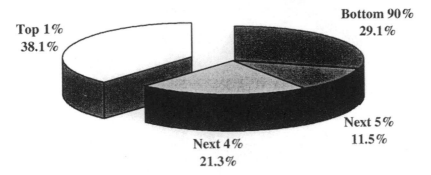

Source: Mishel et al. 2003, 281.

percent of all wealth, more than the combined wealth of the bottom 90 percent of USers. The average net worth of the top 1 percent in 1998 was $10.2 million. If we exclude homes, the predominant form of wealth held by the bottom 90 percent, wealth distribution was even more concentrated in 1998. When we look at just stocks, bonds, and business assets, almost 80 percent of these assets are held by the richest 10 percent of USers. Although millions of USers own stock, the distribution of such ownership is highly concentrated. In 1998 the richest 1 percent owned 53.2 percent of common stock and while the bottom 90 percent owned only 8.9 percent (Mishel et al. 2003, ch. 4).

To qualify in the year 2000 as one of the 400 wealthiest USers (average net worth $3 billion) you had to have a net worth of at least $725 million. The wealthiest individual had a net worth of $63 billion and the combined net worth of these 400 individuals totaled $1.2 trillion.[1] It is here that one can begin to see how private ownership of the means of production concentrates power and control into the hands of relatively few capitalists, so important to the radical political economists' analysis of capitalism.

Income distribution shows a similar pattern of inequality: Table 5.1 shows substantial and growing inequality over this period in the distribution of family income, with larger shares of income going to the richest 20 percent of U.S. families at the expense of

Table 5.1

Shares of Family Income for Selected Years, 1947–2001 (percent)

Year	Lowest fifth	Second fifth	Middle fifth	Fourth fifth	Top fifth	Top 5 %
1947	5.0	11.9	17.0	23.1	43.0	17.5
1973	5.5	11.9	17.5	24.0	41.1	15.5
1989	4.6	10.6	16.5	23.7	44.6	17.9
2001	4.2	9.7	15.5	22.9	47.7	21.0

Source: Mishel et al. (2003, 54).

smaller shares going to the bottom 80 percent of families. Most of the gains have been concentrated in the hands of the richest 5 percent of U.S. families.

This trend toward greater inequality is shown more clearly in Figure 5.2, where the growth of family income is compared for different income groups. The average real incomes of the poorest 20 percent of U.S. families declined by 8.9 percent, from $9613 in 1977 to $8,761 in 1999. In fact, the average incomes of the bottom 60 percent of families fell while the average incomes of the richest 20 percent of American families increased by 33.2 percent in real terms, from $76,834 to $102,308 in 1999. Again, the gains in income for this group were concentrated most heavily in the richest 1 percent U.S. families who saw their after-tax incomes increase on average by 93.4 percent, from $266,629 in 1977 to $515,612 in 1999 (Mishel 2001, p. 58)

Although the intraclass distribution of income is unequal and results from skill differentials and often artificial, capitalist imposed wage differentials, the major factor that accounts for the differences between very high incomes and the rest is property ownership. Income from property ownership represents less than 10 percent for families in the bottom 80 percent and averages 30 percent for the top 20 percent of families. For families in the richest 1 percent, the primary source of income is from property and financial holdings—ownership of the means of production (Mishel et al. 2003, 86).

In the RPE perspective, then, the major source of inequality is

Figure 5.2 **Household After-Tax Real Income Growth, 1977–1999**

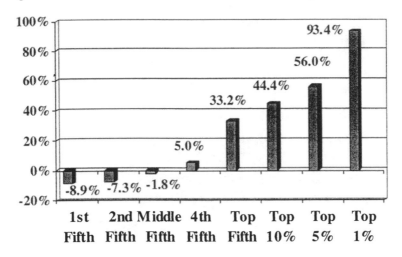

Source: Mishel et al. 2001, 58.

capitalist ownership of the means of production and domination of the labor process. The tremendous degree of inequality is neither at all natural nor predominately the outcome of markets (supply and demand). Although capitalists are constrained to some extent by markets, power is the main determinant of income distribution according to RPE. Employees who have some bargaining power with their employers will do better than those who do not have such power. However, if wages and salaries cut too deeply into the capitalist rate of profit, the safety valve of unemployment (or other capitalist strategies to improve profits at expense of workers discussed in chapter 3) will always restore capitalist control and profits. This ensures low incomes for the majority of workers.

Two decades of capitalist globalization has heightened economic insecurity for working- and middle-class families, which has eroded the bargaining power of workers and resulted in declining real wages for workers, as Figure 5.3 shows. Although working-class real wages started to grow in the mid-1990s, this was after two decades of decline. Furthermore, the increase has been insufficient to raise the level of wages back to their 1973 peak and is

Figure 5.3 **Real Weekly Wages, Production, and Nonsupervisory Workers, 1947–2001** (2001 dollars)

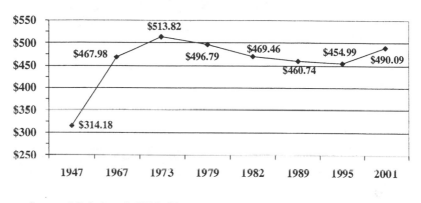

Source: Mishel et al. 2001, 58.

unlikely to do so given the economic recession that began to hit the U.S. economy in year 2000.

In spite of the commonly held view that discrimination is a thing of the past, recent 2001 wage data reveal that economic discrimination against women and people of color remains a significant problem in the United States. The median hourly wage for white men was $15.90, while black men received $11.83, white women $12.07, and black women $10.16 (Mishel et al. 2003, 170–171). In 1967 the ratio to white family median income of black families was 59.2 percent and by 2001 it had changed very little and stood at 62.1 percent. For Hispanic families the income gap has grown more unequal over the last twenty years (Mishel et al. 2003, 41). Women have fared a little better, closing the wage gap somewhat over the last twenty years from 63.1 percent of men's median wages to 78.1 percent. Unfortunately, much of these gains were relative because of falling wages for men rather than substantial wage gains for women (Mishel et al. 2003, 72). Research reveals that much of these differences in wages are the result of economic discrimination (see Albelda et al. 1997; Darity and Mason 1998).

Extensive poverty also characterizes the capitalist distribution of income. In the so-called New Economy of the 1990s, homelessness still existed and poverty rates, although reduced, are still higher in the United States than any other industrialized capitalist country, and millions of USers have no public or private health care coverage. In 2001, about 39 million (11.7 percent of the population) were living below the official government-established poverty line of $18,000 for an urban family of four, an income level radicals and others, including the Bureau of the Census, think is unrealistically low. Even by this standard child poverty rates (16.3 percent) exceed by a substantial margin child poverty rates in other countries. Almost one out of six children under the age of eighteen in the United States is living in poverty (Mishel et al. 2003, 317). By more realistic standards, such as the standard of one-half of the median income used in many other countries, 22 percent of USers are living in poverty (Mishel et al. 2003, 325). In other words, capitalism fails to create sufficient income producing opportunities for over 20 percent of the population.

While many are poor because they cannot get jobs or cannot work (disabled, children, and elderly), most of the poor in the United States who could work, do work either part time or full time. With many part-time jobs and low-paying minimum-wage jobs, capitalism is unable to generate enough jobs that pay a livable wage. In fact, one of the fastest-growing segments of the poor has been the working poor, those who work full or part time in jobs that do not provide living wages. In 2000 earnings provided over 80 percent of the income for poor two-parent families with children and almost 60 percent of income for female-headed families (Schiller 2004, 69–72).

The very large number of poor female-headed families (33.6 percent of female headed families are poor) and the very high percentages of African-Americans and other minorities who are poor (22.7 percent of African-Americans and 21.4 percent of Hispanics were poor in 2001) supports the radical claim that capitalism and discrimination are systemically related (Mishel et al. 2003, 315, 318). These factors, combined with the failure of capitalism to generate enough jobs to go around, account for the high rates of impoverishment in the United States according to radicals.

Poverty is thus treated as a structural rather than an individual problem in RPE.

The substantial degrees of income and wealth inequality, economic discrimination, and poverty support the radical economists' claim that the structural position of capitalists allows them to amass tremendous wealth and income by exploiting the direct producers, the working class, whose necessary consumption is kept at a minimum, leaving great surpluses to be divided among the wealthy elites. This represents one of the greatest contradictions of capitalism, its vast potential to produce abundance for all that is offset by a highly unequal distribution of income and wealth that deprives millions of people of even a decent standard of living.

Globalism and the Capitalist Drive for Profits

The competitive forces inherent in the capitalist organization of production propel capitalists in an endless search for higher rates of profits. These forces drive capitalists beyond national boundaries in search of additional markets, cheaper raw materials, a cheaper and more exploitable workforce, and more profitable investment opportunities. Although such forces have driven capitalists beyond national borders since sixteenth-century European colonialism, the heightened pace of the internationalization of capital at the end of the twentieth century has given rise to notions of globalization. Radicals tend view this more recent stage of global expansion as a continuation of one of the inherent dynamic tendencies of a capitalist economic system.

Radicals thus view capitalism as an inherently expansionary system. The spread of capitalism has meant that to fully understand capitalism, one must view it as a world system linked together by capitalist markets and investment. The fates of different countries and peoples are thus tied to the global dynamics of capitalism, heavily influenced by the advanced, dominant capitalist countries such as the United States.

In the United States almost all of the 500 largest corporations are multinational, and much if not most of their profits are derived from foreign sales and operations. The foreign expansion of U.S. capitalism after World War II was accompanied and facilitated by U.S. political and military hegemony over much of the rest of the world, keeping it open to and safe for U.S. capital.

At home U.S. capital is able to more easily dominate both the economy and other spheres of society such as ideology and government than it can abroad. Capitalists have much greater difficulty insuring the proper business climate in other countries given the national sovereignty of these countries. Imperialism is the concept used in RPE to characterize the economic and political relations between the United States and other nations. Imperialist relations include direct and indirect actions taken by and on behalf of multinational corporations to manipulate and control the economy, government, and culture of another country.

Such relations include economic, political, and military intervention by the U.S. government into the sovereign affairs of other nations on behalf of U.S. corporate interests. Any country that tries to regulate, control, or restrict the activities of U.S. capital in its country risks economic and political sanctions. U.S. government and corporate domination of international economic institutions such as the International Monetary Fund (IMF), World Bank, and World Trade Organization (WTO) keeps the world system functioning in the best interests of corporate capitalism. Direct military intervention is often resorted to. This includes overthrowing democratically elected governments (Iran 1953, Guatemala 1954, and Chile 1972), covert intervention to influence political outcomes (Jamaica 1978), and the support of ruthless dictatorships (Reza Shah Pahlavi in Iran, Augusto Pinochet in Chile, Ferdinand Marcos in the Philippines, Park Chung Hee in South Korea, and the Somoza family in Nicaragua) that give free rein to multinational corporations to exploit their country's resources and people without restraint. Direct military intervention has also been used to bring recalcitrant nations into line (Afghanistan, Iraq, Nicaragua, Guatemala, Grenada, Panama, Vietnam).

As a result of imperialist domination of other nations, capitalists are able to maintain high rates of profit by exploiting the resources and peoples of other countries, particularly Third World countries. The impact of the spread of capitalism to these countries, which began with colonialism and continues today with neocolonialism, has, according to RPE analysis, been largely negative. The economic surplus generated in Third World countries has largely accrued to foreign capital through unequal trade,[2] foreign ownership of Third World assets (factories, plantations, mines, and natural resources), and foreign domination of technology, marketing, and financial markets.

Although some economic growth has resulted in Third World countries and even industrialization in a few countries (e.g., Taiwan, South Korea) from capitalist expansion, the overall impact of foreign capital has distorted development and generated what radicals call underdevelopment. While parts (enclaves) of Third World countries experience rapid economic growth and some people benefit from foreign capital, such development is shallow, leaving most regions and people languishing in abject poverty.

High rates of unemployment and underemployment in the Third World means workers have little to no bargaining power. Repressive governments, often with U.S. assistance, keep unions out by using military force (and U.S.-supplied arms) if necessary to suppress striking workers. With a surplus of labor and people who live on the edge of starvation, foreign capitalists are able to pay extremely low wages that are a small fraction of U.S. wages. Workers are also willing to accept long hours, sweatshop working conditions, and a pace of work that leaves workers exhausted at the end of the day. Increasingly, the subsidiaries of U.S. multinational corporations hire only female labor because of their socially internalized passivity and docility, the product of patriarchal Third World cultures. The result: much lower costs and higher rates of profits for U.S. corporations, and the continuing poverty and oppression of Third World people.

The domestic linkages that have fostered rapid capitalist development in the United States are missing in the Third World. The positive stimuli created by foreign capitalists are externalized in the Third World, fostering continued corporate expansion outside the Third World. Low wages, imported capital goods, and the use of U.S. citizens in management positions means that too little domestic demand is generated from the activities of U.S. multinational corporations in Third World countries.

The economic surplus generated by foreign capital is a potential source of new investment. However, given the low level of domestic demand in much of the Third World, markets are quickly saturated and the surplus is reinvested elsewhere. These capital outflows from the Third World take the form of repatriated profits, royalties, interest payments, and licensing fees and leave these countries underdeveloped. Such outflows from the Third World generate perpetual balance-of-payments deficits and have paved the way for the debt crisis now plaguing much of the Third World.

Radicals advance another cause that promotes surplus drain and underdevelopment in the Third World. In the advanced capitalist countries, the rapid accumulation of capital and industrialization did not take place until the precapitalist relations and organization of production had been replaced by capitalist forms. (See discussion of the transition from feudalism to capitalism and the discussion of the primitive accumulation of capital on in chapter 1.) The expansion of capitalism into the Third World has tended to strengthen rather than weaken these precapitalist relations of production that act as a further barrier blocking economic development in the Third World. Although preserving precapitalist relations of production has blocked successful economic development, it has enabled foreign capital to dominate Third World countries.

The heightened globalization from 1980 to the present has, in the radical economic view, both increased the exploitation of workers around the world and intensified labor in the United States as workers are forced to work harder and longer for less pay. As we will see in the next section, globalism, the uneven development of capitalism in different countries, and the underdevelopment of the Third World play important parts in the RPE analysis of economic crises.

Capitalism and Cyclical Economic Crisis

As we have seen, the competitive drive for profits in capitalism creates powerful forces of change. The process of capital accumulation is not smooth, however, and the resulting uneven rate of change creates perpetual boom and bust cycles. The macrodynamics of the capitalist economy is linked very closely to the amount of investment, which depends upon the expected rate of profit in the United States and in the rest of the world. Therefore, conditions in the world capitalist economy are important to understand the macroeconomic dynamics in any particular country.

Short-Run Dynamics

Radicals for the most part rely on a short-run theory that is essentially based on John Maynard Keynes. It is more faithful to the original theory advanced by Keynes than the variant found in orthodox textbooks. In the short run, output and employment are determined by the aggregate demand for goods and service. Fluctuations in total demand, according to radicals, stem primarily from fluctuations in investment, a component of demand. Investment in the United States depends upon the expected rate of profit in the United States as well as the rest of world. If the expected rate of profit is higher abroad, then capitalists will invest outside the country. Total demand will be less and consequently there will be less output and employment than if capitalists had invested in the United States.

The determination of employment is also somewhat different in RPE. Labor supply is determined by the size of the population and labor force participation rates which are determined by economic and cultural forces (attitudes towards work) exerted on families and workers. Labor demand is determined by a very different set of forces, economic forces exerted on employers. In the short run, the total demand for goods and services determines the amount of utilized capital (*CG in use*). The ratio of labor employed to utilized capital will establish the demand for labor.

It would be coincidental if the number of people looking for jobs was equal to the number of jobs being offered by employers. In the classical view, held by many neoclassical economists today, if there are more people looking for work at the current wage than there are jobs available, a lower wage will bring labor supply into equilibrium with labor demand. In RPE, wage cutting can have the opposite effect. This is called the paradox of wage cutting. If all workers get paid less, this could result in less consumer spending and a worsening in expected demand by capitalists. Given that the demand for labor time is a derived demand, wage cutting can lead to greater unemployment rather than less. Wages thus enter the determination of profits twice: once as a cost of production and again as a source of demand.

We can show this graphically using aggregate labor supply and demand curves (see Figure 5.4). LS is the labor supply and LD_1 is the labor demand curve. The labor demand curve is drawn assuming other things constant, such as the aggregate demand for goods and services. LD_1 indicates that as long as total goods and services demanded is unchanged, employers will hire more workers if wages are lower. At an initial wage of W_1, there would be unemployment equal to DS measured on the horizontal axis.

In RPE, cutting wages to W_2 would not bring about a full employment equilibrium, as it is assumed to do in neoclassical theory, because lower wages mean less consumption by workers and therefore less aggregate demand for goods and services. This causes a downward shift in labor demand from LD_1 to LD_2 as employers reduce their demand for labor at all wage levels as result of their adjusted sales expectations. In this case, with LD_2 labor demand and a wage of W_2, unemployment has actually increased to $D'S'$!

The actual outcome would depend upon the elasticity of labor supply and demand as well as the size of the shift in demand. Radicals argue that it is realistic to assume that the labor supply curve is very inelastic (workers do not change very much the number of hours they are willing to work in response to changes in wages). They also assume that wage cuts will cause large shifts in aggregate demand (75 percent of consumption comes out of wages/

Figure 5.4 **Aggregate Labor Demand and Supply**

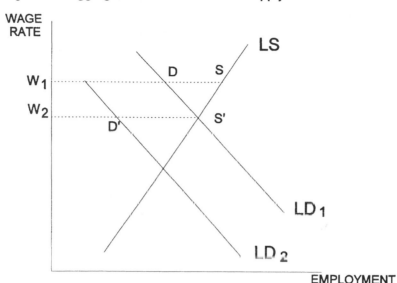

salaries) Although investment demand may be stimulated by wage cuts, radicals assume that it is unlikely to offset the fall in consumer demand. Adding this theory to the safety value theory (see chapter 3, "Rate of Profit" subsection) gives a strong basis for the radical claim that unemployment is a more or less permanent feature of capitalism. We will see below how employment levels can affect economic cycles.

Medium-Term Dynamics

Most of RPE theorizing focuses on medium- and long-run cycles, which distinguish RPE from the short-period emphasis common in orthodox macroeconomics. These cycles are in the RPE view the product of capitalism, not just aberrations correctable by public policy. This approach starts from a premise of instability rather than one of stability and full employment, the starting point of neoclassical microeconomic theory.

The medium-run cycle, or business cycle, is a three- to five-year cycle during which the economy goes through an expansion phase followed by a recession or contraction phase. Following

Bowles and Edwards (1993, ch. 15), employment levels play a dominant role in the cyclical behavior of the U.S. economy. Unemployment creates the environment necessary to resolve the conflict between employers and workers in a way that maintains high profits for capitalists.

The expected rate of profit (r) is determined by the expected capacity utilization rate (cu) and the expected profit rate on utilized capital (ru) where

$ru = f$ (cost conditions of the firm)
$cu = f$ (demand conditions of the firm)

Demand conditions affect the expected utilization rate (cu) and cost conditions affect the expected profit rate on capital (ru). The level of unemployment will affect both. Increasing unemployment will lower the demand for goods and services, and thus lower expected cu (negative effect on expected profit rate). As previously discussed (see unit labor costs in the "Production and Conflict in Capitalism" section of chapter 3) greater unemployment will lower wages and/or increase the intensity of labor (d), both of which will lower unit labor costs and thus increase the expected ru (positive effect on expected profit rate).

The overall effect on the expected rate of profit depends upon which of these opposing conditions dominates, and that depends upon the phase of the business cycle. During the expansion period, high expected profits produce high rates of investment as capitalists rush to take advantage of profitable investment opportunities. This eventually generates high demand for labor and low unemployment, creating the conditions for higher wages and lower labor intensity. Additionally, greater demand for raw materials and loanable funds by both consumers and corporations puts more pressure on costs as the prices of materials and interest rates rise. Cyclical inflation begins to appear as capitalists attempt to maintain their profit rates by raising product prices.

At the peak of the cycle profit rates are squeezed from the cost side. Additionally, the growth in productive capacity from the expansion outraces the growth in total demand, causing a drop in capacity utilization rates. With both lower rates of profit and excess capacity, expected ru and expected cu are low-producing, low-expected rates of profit. Capitalists respond by cutting output, laying off workers, and investing less, slowing the rate of capital accumulation. This intensifies demand problems and the downturn in a few industries spreads to other industries.

During the contraction period workers continue to be laid off and unemployment grows. Wages drop (or fail to keep up with increases in productivity) and capitalist control of the labor process increases and labor intensity rises. As the demand for raw materials and loans slackens, materials prices and interest rates fall. Excess inventories are sold off. At the pit of the cycle cost conditions are favorable for high rates of profit, so that expected ru is high. Demand is low and capacity utilization is low. However, cyclical inflation is low, making U.S. goods more attractive to the rest of the world, and people/businesses who have put off purchases are waiting for incomes to rise so expected cu is also high.

Anticipating higher profits, capitalists begin expanding output and investment, increasing the rate of capital accumulation, and another expansion phase begins. Capitalism, driven by competition and the rate of profit, relies upon business cycles and unemployment to maintain high rates of profit and the accumulation of capital. Full employment, steady growth, and a stable price level are desirable goals, but impossible to sustain, according to radicals, in a capitalist system.

Government intervention to maintain high levels of total demand at the peak of the cycle while benefiting workers exacerbates the cost squeeze on capitalist profits. This generates higher rates of inflation as capitalists raise prices to keep profits high. Inflation is destabilizing, particularly for financial capitalists and those engaged in foreign markets where currency stability is necessary to maintain competitive positions.

Given capitalist domination of the state and ideology, discussed in chapter 4, economic policy debates will tend to favor the interests of capital not labor. The blame for inflation will be placed on workers, unions, and excessive government intervention and spending.

Business pressures will insure government fiscal and monetary policies consistent with the accumulation needs of the business community. The resulting unemployment will be rationalized with theories such as the natural rate of employment, which argue that whatever the rate of unemployment happens to be is "natural" and that workers are unemployed only because their wage demands are out of line with the market or because they lack marketable skills (structural unemployment).

A misbehaved cycle is when for some reason the economy fails to cycle normally through its successive phases. Government intervention to prolong the peak is one example. Also workers might be able to resist wage cuts and speedup in the contraction phase if labor organization is strong. The inflation generated by a misbehaved cycle is called structural inflation in RPE. In this view, evidence of a misbehaved cycle usually signifies some long-term structural problem.

As we saw in chapter 3 unemployment is just one way that the conflict between capitalists and workers can be resolved. Social democracy and authoritarianism are other ways of resolving these conflicts. Sweden has been able historically to maintain low rates of unemployment (averaging 2 percent or less), without affecting the capitalist rate of profit, using a social democratic mediation regime. An authoritarian regime accomplishes the same task in a country like South Korea using repressive methods. Both of these mediation regimes produce more stable economic outcomes for capitalists. With more stable rates of profits, layoffs are unnecessary to restore profits and medium-term cyclical amplitude is dampened considerably when compared to the United States.

Although different regimes of mediation are possible within capitalism, the conflict generated by the contradictory positions of employers and workers in the capitalist organization of production remains a constant source of conflict and potential instability. Even in Sweden capitalism has succumbed to the pressure of global capitalist forces. There remain very powerful long-run tendencies in capitalism that produce cycles even more disruptive of the status quo.

Long-Run Dynamics

The analysis of long-term growth and stagnation by radicals is quite complex and captures several long-term cyclical trends in capitalist accumulation. These cyclical trends extend anywhere from thirty to fifty years, marking the boundaries of major historical phases or stages of capitalist development (see chapter 2, Table 2.2).

Given the difficulty of analyzing such long-term trends, where everything is subject to change, it is not surprising to find that there is a fair amount of disagreement among radical economists concerning the exact cause of the long-run cyclical behavior of capitalism. At the theoretical level, radicals have identified several tendencies generated within capitalism with the potential to cause major long-term disruptions of the accumulation process. Although there are some theoretical disagreements here, the major source of disagreement among radicals is over which tendency tends to dominate at any particular moment in the long-run cyclical behavior of capitalism. This question is largely an empirical one and it is here that one understandably finds much disagreement among radicals given the magnitude and difficulty of such long-run studies. (On theoretical differences see Norton 1992.)

In the discussion that follows, we will not focus on these differences but will limit our discussion to the primary RPE theoretical analysis of causal factors underlying the long-run cyclical behavior of capitalism. The causal factors include the rising organic composition of capital, social conflict, underconsumption, and financial structure. All of these factors are systemically caused by the capitalist organization of production, and taken together they provide a powerful basis for the explanation of recurrent structural crises in capitalism.[3]

Tendency for the Rate of Profit to Fall

This tendency is the result of the capitalist propensity to mechanize production. The organic composition of capital measures the degree to which capitalists use fixed capital. As a result of competitive forces in capitalism, firms are compelled to increase productivity and lower costs. Technological change plays an important part in the competitive struggle for profits among capitalists. This drive to increase productivity leads to the use of greater amounts of fixed capital (mechanization and automation) per unit of output.

Individual capitalists first to innovate are able to both lower their unit costs and lower their prices while making a higher rate of profit than their competitors. This competitive advantage will be short-lived, however, as other capitalists are compelled to follow suit and adopt the new technology. As they do, the average rate of profit for the economy as a whole is driven down. Thus technological strategies, while they improve the rate of profit in the short run for a few individual capitalists, produce a contradictory tendency for the economywide rate of profit to fall for all capitalists in the long run.

The long-run tendency for the overall rate of profit to fall is caused by the rising organic composition of capital that in the radical view necessitates a lower rate of profit.[4] Given that capitalism runs on profit, a secular decline in the rate of profit means less profit for the capitalist class and investment cutbacks. This generates excess capacity and workers will be laid off in large numbers, creating an economic crisis.

There are a number of counteracting tendencies that can prolong the onset of such a crisis, such as greater exploitation of workers or foreign expansion, but none can in the radical perspective completely overcome this capitalist tendency toward periodic economic crises. During such crises there is great economic and social turmoil (business and bank failures, widespread unemployment and social dislocation) such as the Great Depression. Like medium-term cycles, in the long run economic crises eventually restore the conditions for profitable capital accumulation, paving the way for another period of economic expansion.

Social Structure of Accumulation

The second underlying factor identified by some radicals as causing long-run economic crises is the social conflict produced by capitalism. We have seen previously that in the radical perspective ownership of the means of production gives capitalists the legal right to command the labor process. However, the degree of capitalist success (measured by the rate of profit) depends upon the power that capitalists wield over workers. It also depends upon the exercise of power in intercapitalist relations (domestic and foreign), and relations with the state and other nations.

Social conflict in any of these relationships can be destabilizing and interrupt the accumulation process. For the capitalist economy to function, a complementary set of supportive institutions is required to mediate these conflicts in ways that provide sufficient stability and profits for the expanded reproduction of capital. This external environment is referred to by radicals as the social structures of accumulation (SSA), a concept introduced in chapter 2.

The forces of change inherent in the accumulation process generate powerful destabilizing forces that alter the balance of power and undermine the SSA, causing an economic crisis. The resolution of such a crisis requires a new SSA to mediate the social conflicts generated by the changed economic environment in a way that reestablishes the conditions for the steady accumulation of capital.

The best way to illustrate the way that social conflict generates long-run cyclical decline is to discuss briefly the post–World War II SSA in the United States. Radicals identify four principal buttresses of U.S. postwar capitalist power, each of which involved a particular set of institutionalized power relations giving U.S. corporations the control and stability they needed for long-run accumulation. These arrangements are referred to as the (1) capital-labor accord, (2) Pax Americana, (3) capital-citizen accord, and (4) limitation of inter-capitalist rivalry. Together these made up the postwar SSA. In the RPE perspective this SSA provided the framework for success, promoting capitalist growth and accumulation in the United States after World War II.

The capital-labor accord embraced a set of institutions and agreements involving an explicit and implicit quid pro quo between employers and workers that assured management control over

enterprise decision making with union submission and cooperation. In exchange, workers (particularly unionized workers) were
promised rising real wages in tandem with labor productivity, improved working conditions, and greater job security. The accord
was enforced by unions on the one hand, and by a bureaucratic
and hierarchical system of labor management on the other. The
postwar capital-labor accord resolved potentially disruptive disputes, allowing capitalists to pursue corporate profit-maximizing
strategies with minimal resistance from workers.

Pax Americana included the structure of international economic
and political relations that assured U.S. corporations a dominant
role in the world capitalist economy. These institutions included
the institutions formed by the 1946 Bretton Woods agreement
which established the U.S. dollar as the key international currency,
making Wall Street the banking center of the capitalist world. The
International Monetary Fund, General Agreement on Tariffs and
Trade (GATT), and the World Bank gave effective hegemony over
the world economy to the United States that dominated these organizations. The world economy was thus regulated in ways favorable to the United States. The terms of trade between U.S.
capitalists and foreign buyers and sellers favored the United States.

Barriers to the free flow of capital were removed, allowing U.S.
corporations to invest and move plants practically anywhere in
the world. The Cold War and acceptance of an anticommunist ideology paved the way for a worldwide U.S. military presence that
while it may have protected the "free world" from Soviet expansion also protected "free markets" from those who would restrict
the activities of U.S. corporations. Pax Americana thus provided
U.S. capitalists with cheap raw materials and intermediate products imported from other countries. It also provided corporations
with foreign markets for their products as well as outlets for capital investment where labor was cheap. Potentially disruptive international conflicts were mediated in favor of U.S. capitalists.
This facilitated rapid foreign expansion by U.S. corporations and
high profits, both of which in part account for the rapid accumulation of capital in the United States following World War II.

The capital-citizen accord represented a set of political arrangements that mediated the conflict over public policy so that meeting the needs of citizens was constrained by the principle of capitalist profitability. Corporate interests dominated both political parties. The then-dominant Democratic Party included organized labor as a junior partner. Policies to meet the economic needs of citizens were limited to the New Deal legislation that guaranteed minimal security from old age, disability, and unemployment. Funded largely from taxes on the working class, these policies had little effect on capitalist profitability. The low level of security preserved the high cost of unemployment to workers and helped maintain capitalists' power over workers.

The anticommunist ideology used effectively to justify foreign military expansion was also used to purge the United States of domestic elements thought to be communist. Under the leadership of Senator Joseph McCarthy in the early 1950s, anyone who challenged the status quo in the United States, particularly those in the labor movement, education, media, and government, was suspect. Even though most were not communists, hundreds of people's lives were ruined, effectively purging the United States of those who might challenge the status quo, particularly the corporate community. The anticommunist ideology and McCarthyism made citizens fearful of expressing any dissent, providing an important underpinning of the postwar capital-citizen accord. This accord, in the radical view, effectively constrained potential political conflict in favor of corporate domination.

The last pillar of the postwar structure of accumulation was the moderation of intercapitalist rivalry. Following the war U.S. corporations found themselves with few competitors. The war-torn economies of most other industrialized countries left U.S. corporations with unchallenged access to world markets. The rapid accumulation of capital after the war meant that domestically U.S corporations could grow and maintain high rates of profit with little concern for domestic competition. What competition there was in the domestic U.S. economy was kept within the boundaries of the secondary sector of the dual economy, effectively shielding the large, primary-sector corporations from competition. The diminution of both domestic and international capitalist rivalries created further stability for U.S. corporate expansion and accumulation.

In this radical perspective, these important institutional components combine to make up the postwar SSA, which facilitated and promoted high profits and the stability necessary for long-term accumulation. The SSA is one of the major determinants of the pace of investment and growth. The power relations mediating capitalists' interactions with workers, other capitalists, and citizens affect the rate of profit. Radicals refer to this as the "battlefront conditions of a three-front war." The institutions of the SSA shape capitalist power and the rate of accumulation. The postwar SSA mediated social conflict in ways favorable to capitalist domination and stability. The result was one of the longest, most robust periods of capitalist accumulation in U.S. history.

However, the very success of capitalist growth undermines the basis for expansion. According to these radicals, the postwar SSA eroded during the period 1966–1973. Capitalist prosperity generates stresses and strains that adversely affect the rate of profit. The capital-labor accord began to break down as workers tired of bureaucratic control and the high rate of industrial accidents brought about by the rapid pace of production. With low unemployment, employers' power diminished and workers began resisting by striking for better conditions of work.

Pax Americana began to unravel as other countries challenged U.S. economic, political, and military hegemony, prompted by the stresses and strains produced by the U.S. corporate-led growth of the world capitalist economy. Third World countries began to resist U.S. domination and in the case of South Vietnam dragged the United States into a major war that was subsequently lost by the United States. Raw material exporters took greater control of their own resources, the most visible example of which was the Organization of Petroleum Exporting Countries (OPEC), shifting the terms of trade to its advantage, at the expense of oil consumers and to the benefit of multinational oil companies whose profits soared.

The rapidly growing world economy soon outgrew the international monetary system, leading to its dramatic collapse in 1972 when the United States unilaterally suspended convertibility of the U.S. dollar to gold.

Unbridled corporate growth and expansion created many pressures that upset the capital-citizen accord. When capitalist profits are the sole guide to growth, social costs proliferate and unchecked they impose significant hardship on citizens. Citizens organized themselves politically to challenge corporate domination with new government regulations affecting traffic safety, occupational health and safety, environmental protection, consumer product safety, and nuclear power generation. The uneven benefits of capitalist growth meant that many USers failed to benefit, leaving millions impoverished. Citizens' movements sought to eliminate poverty through government programs, and the civil rights and the women's liberation movements sought to limit discrimination through civil rights and antidiscrimination legislation.

Finally, the very success of postwar capitalist expansion intensified intercapitalist rivalry. The rebuilding of the war-torn economies after the war gave rise to foreign competition challenging U.S. corporations in the world economy. At home rivalries between U.S. corporations intensified with an increase in merger activity.

As a result of these combined pressures, the postwar SSA fell apart and U.S. capitalists began adopting new profit strategies aimed at reasserting their domination. However, the power of workers, foreigners, and citizens was strong enough to hold capitalists off. The result was a political stalemate that accounts for the misbehaved business cycles of the 1970s and consequent stagflation: high rates of inflation combined with high rates of unemployment. Corporations unable to keeps profits high any other way had to resort to raising product prices. Table 5.2 summarizes these changes.

This stalemate was not broken in the radical view until 1980 and the election of the probusiness, antilabor Reagan administration. Made possible by the unity of corporate capitalists, with the support of the middle classes, government rolled back regulations,

Table 5.2

The Rise and Demise of the Postwar Social Structure of Accumulation

Phase	Capital-labor accord	Pax Americana	Capital-citizen accord	Intercapitalist rivalry
Boom: 1948–1966	Cost of job loss rises; workers' resistance down	U.S. military dominance; terms of trade improve	Government support for accumulation; profits main state priority	Corporations insulated from domestic and foreign competition
Erosion: 1966–1973	Cost of job loss plunges; workers' resistance spreads	Military power challenged; terms of trade hold steady	Citizens' movements take hold	Foreign competition and domestic mergers begin to affect corporations
Stalemate: 1973–1979	Stagnant economy creates stalemate between capital and labor	OPEC and fall in US$ result in decline in terms of trade	Citizens' movements effect new fetters on business	Pressure of foreign competition and domestic rivalry intensifies

Source: From David Gordon et al. "Power, Accumulation and Crisis: The Rise and Demise of the Postwar Social Structure of Accumulation," in *The Imperial Economy. Book I: Macroeconomics from a Left Perspective,* ed. Robert Cherry et al. (Riverside, CA: Union for Radical Political Economics, 1987), 51. Reprinted with permission from the Union for Radical Political Economics.

taxes, and programs costly to capitalists. With higher average rates of unemployment in the 1980s, corporations were able to reassert their domination over workers, driving wages and benefits down, and forcing workers to accept speedup and other corporate-dictated conditions of work. Corporate union-busting strategies were also instrumental in regaining capitalist domination of the workplace.

This paved the way for a rather dramatic restructuring of corporate capitalism and, through a process of market and financial deregulation, deindustrialization, corporate downsizing, and globalization (neoliberalism), corporate capitalists were able to restore corporate dominance and profitability at the expense of workers who faced much higher costs of job loss. There is debate among radicals about whether or not these efforts created a new SSA capable of facilitating another long-run period of capitalist growth and accumulation. While high rates of profit were restored and growth took place in the 1980s, radicals argued that compared to previous long-term expansions, growth was relatively weak and was at the expense of stagnant and declining real incomes of the majority of U.S. families. Furthermore, the competitiveness of U.S. capitalists in the world economy was extremely weak during the 1980s (Bowles et al. 1989; Bluestone and Harrison 1988).

Following the recession in the early 1990s, the U.S. economy rebounded with a long period of growth, low inflation, low unemployment, and rising stock market prices. The unexpected robustness of the U.S. economy was attributed to what were believed to be significant structural changes that became popularly labeled as the "New Economy." The basis for the New Economy was rapid growth of telecommunications, computerization, and the dot-com industry. Radical economists accept the reality of many of these changes in the contemporary U.S. economy, but they argue that they do not constitute a "New Economy"; rather just the continuation of capitalism complete with all its problems and contradictions (see *Monthly Review* "Special Issue" 2001).

Whether or not a new SSA has evolved is not clear; if so it could be labeled the "Neoliberal" social structure of accumulation, one that is decidedly more favorable to capitalists than the working class. Although the 1990s economic gains were real enough, particularly for corporate capitalists, the existing structures of accumulation have worked to the disadvantage of much of the working class and many within the middle classes as real wages and incomes, despite some improvement in the late 1990s, have remained below their 1973 peak. Economic insecurity remains high and U.S. workers find themselves putting in more time on the job than their counterparts in other advanced industrial countries.

Whether or not as we move through the twenty-first century a new SSA will evolve to reverse these trends is problematic. It depends upon the strengths of competing interests and their struggles to enact changes. In the RPE such conflicts are determined in large degree by the structurally imposed class conflicts between workers and capitalists. In these ways social conflict shapes the long-run cyclical behavior of capitalism.

Underconsumption

The ability of capitalists to keep profits high by forcing the incomes of working people down can be contradictory in capitalism. If incomes do not keep pace with the increased capacity generated by capital accumulation, then capitalists will be unable to sell all they can produce. Radicals call this a realization crisis and it results in the third potential cause of long-run cyclical decline, underconsumption.

Some radicals argue that workers are permanently disadvantaged relative to capitalists given the structural organization of capitalism. Wages will, except in unusual circumstances, be less than labor productivity, generating large surpluses for capitalists. The reinvestment of this surplus generates productive capacity that tends to exceed total demand normally restricted by low wages. Unable to sell all that is produced, capitalists are forced to cut back production and lay off workers, causing further reductions in demand.

The result is economic stagnation, which according to some radicals is a more or less permanent state of capitalism, its advanced, monopoly stage. The rise of the large, monopolistic corporation enhanced the power of corporate capitalists to achieve high rates of profit. This produces a tendency for the surplus to rise in this phase of capitalism. However, so much surplus is generated that capitalists have difficulty absorbing the surplus in ways that maintain high rates of profit. Stagnation is the result unless there are counteracting forces such as wars, military spending, credit expansion, or epoch-making innovations that stimulate growth and investment.

Such events are unpredictable and occur irregularly, and account for some of the long-run periods of expansion experienced by capitalism. Some radical economists believe that record levels of consumer debt fueled much of the economic expansion in the so-called New Economy of the 1990s, a level of debt that by the year 2000 could no longer be sustained. This brought a return of economic stagnation, explained in this case by underconsumption, believed to be a natural state of advanced monopoly capitalism.

Fragile Financial Structure

A final cause of long-run cycles in capitalism is created by the financial structure that regulates the supply of money and credit. The need for money and credit in a capitalist economy is tied to the accumulation process. If the supply of money and credit is either too little or too great for the needs of capital accumulation, economic expansion can be halted. Financial capitalists are driven by the same need to maximize profits as industrial capitalists. There is no mechanism to insure that the provision of money and credit will be advanced in amounts sufficient to guarantee long-term capital accumulation.

According to radicals, the control of the money supply is largely outside the hands of a central bank (in the case of the United States the Federal Reserve). In this view, credit creation is not predictable or regular, as relatively unconstrained multinational banks and other credit-creating institutions are driven by their own competitive strategies for profit making. Capitalist financial structures are fragile and have a tendency to overextend credit during periods of long-run expansion, threatening financial collapse and economic crisis, and offer too little credit during periods of stagnation stifling economic expansion.

For example, in the face of falling profits (perhaps due to a rising organic composition of capital or an eroding SSA) corporations may be forced·to borrow to continue accumulation and remain competitive. If debt continues to grow, borrowing may be necessary to pay off past debt, which the financial system is only too willing to provide in order to protect past loans. In such a situation a normal downturn in the business cycle can cause corporate bankruptcies and financial panic as loans fall into default, threatening a collapse of the financial system. An example of such a collapse was the stock market crash in 1929. Under these circumstances what starts out as a normal business cycle recession winds up as a long-term economic crisis, halting long-run capital accumulation.

Radicals who emphasize the financial structure point to the record levels of current U.S. corporate, consumer, and foreign debt as well as the Third World debt crises, such as the Mexico peso crisis of 1994 and the Asian financial crisis of 1997, which threatened a financial collapse and long-term economic crisis of the world capitalist system.

In summary, capitalism is thus viewed in RPE as a dynamic system with much potential for rapid growth and economic expansion. While the dynamics of capitalism advance society quite rapidly, it is not without important flaws or contradictions. Significant poverty, inequality, imperialism, and periodic economic and social disruption plague capitalism. When added to the oppressive nature of the capitalist-organized workplace and labor process, capitalism emerges as a highly inefficient and unjust system. It is to this assessment that we turn to in the next chapter and the alternatives to capitalism proposed by radicals.

Notes

1. The 400 richest USers are listed and profiled in the October issue of *Forbes* magazine every year. This elite group is referred to as the "Forbes 400." The Forbes 400 can be researched at www.Forbes.com.

2. Trade between countries where productivity is similar but rates of return to labor and capital are different. For a discussion of the mechanism of unequal trade see Koont (1987).

3. The following discussion is drawn from Cherry et al. (1988), especially the articles by James Devine, Anwar Shaikh, David Gordon et al., John Bellamy Foster, and Robert Pollin.

4. The logic of this argument is based on the labor theory of value and for the sake of brevity is not developed here. For a complete explanation see Shaikh (1978a, 1978b).

References

Albelda, Randy, Robert Drago, and Steve Shulman. 1997. *Unlevel Playing Field: Understanding Wage Inequality and Discrimination.* Cambridge, MA: Economic Affairs Bureau.

Bluestone, Barry, and Bennett Harrison. 1988. *The Great U-Turn: Corporate Restructuring and the Polarization of America.* New York: Basic Books.

Bowles, Samuel, et al. 1989. "Business Ascendancy and Economic Impasse: A Structural Perspective on Conservative Economics." *Journal of Economic Perspectives* 3, no. 1: 107–134.

Bowles, and Richard Edwards. 1993. *Understanding Capitalism.* New York: HarperCollins.

Cherry, Robert et al., eds. 1988. *The Imperiled Economy Book I: Macroeconomics from a Left Perspective.* Riverside, CA: Union for Radical Political Economics.

Darity, William, and Patrick Mason. 1998. "Evidence on Discrimination in Employment: Codes of Color, Codes of Gender." *Journal of Economics Perspectives* 12, no. 2 (Spring): 63–90.

Edwards, Richard, Michael Reich, and Thomas Weisskopf, eds. 1986. *The Capitalist System.* 3d ed. Englewood Cliffs, NJ: Prentice-Hall.

Koont, Sinan. 1987. "Three Essays in Economic Theory: Unequal Exchange, Shortage Based Macro Growth Model of a Socialist Economy, and Foreign Trade Policy in Centrally Planned Economies." Unpublished dissertation, University of Massachusetts, Amherst.

Mishel, Lawrence, Jared Bernstein, and Heather Boushey. 2003 *State of Working America 2002/2003.* Ithaca, NY: Cornell University Press.

Mishel, Lawrence, Jared Bernstein, and John Schmitt. 2001. *The State of Working America 2000/2001.* Ithaca, NY: Cornell University Press.

Norton, Bruce. 1992. "Radical Theories of Accumulation and Crisis: Development and Directions." In *Radical Economics*, ed. Bruce Roberts and Susan Feiner, 155–193. Boston: Kluwer Academic.

Schiller, Bradley R. 2004. *The Economics of Poverty and Discrimination.* 9th ed. Upper Saddle River, NJ: Pearson Prentice-Hall.

Shaikh, Anwar. 1978a. "An Introduction to the History of Crisis Theories." In *U.S. Capitalism in Crisis*, 232–235. New York: Union for Radical Political Economics.

————. 1978b. "Political Economy and Capitalism: Notes on Dobb's Theory Crisis." *Cambridge Journal of Economics* 2, no. 2: 233–251.
"Special Issue: The New Economy: Myth and Reality." 2001. *Monthly Review* 52, no. 11 (April).

Further Reading

Inequality and Poverty

Block, Fred et al. 1987. *The Mean Season: The Attack on the Welfare State.* New York: Pantheon.
Brouwer, Steve. 1998. *Sharing the Pie: A Citizens Guide to Wealth and Power in America.* New York: Henry Holt.
Collins, Chuck, and Felice Yeskel. 2000. *Economic Apartheid: A Primer on Economic Inequality and Insecurity.* New York: The New Press.
Collins, Chuck et al. 1999. *Shifting Fortunes: The Perils of the Growing American Wealth Gap.* Boston: United for a Fair Economy.
Edwards, Richard, Michael Reich, and Thomas Weisskopf, eds. 1986. *The Capitalist System.* 3d ed. Englewood Cliffs, NJ: Prentice-Hall, ch. 6.
Mishel, Lawrence, Jared Bernstein, and Heather Boushey. 2003. *The State of Working America 2002/2003.* Ithaca, NY: Cornell University Press.
Reiman, Jeffrey. 1998. *The Rich Get Richer and the Poor Get Prison: Ideology, Class, and Criminal Justice.* 5th ed. Boston: Allyn and Bacon.
Rodgers, Harrell R. Jr. 2000. *American Poverty in a New Era of Reform.* Armonk, NY: M.E. Sharpe.
Rubin, Lillian B. 1994. *Families on the Fault Line: America's Working Class Speaks About the Family, the Economy, Race, and Ethnicity.* New York: HarperCollins.
Sherman, Howard J. 1987. *Foundations of Radical Political Economy.* Armonk, NY: M.E. Sharpe, ch. 4.

Globalism and Imperialism

Amin, Samir. 1977. *Unequal Development.* New York: Monthly Review Press.
Anderson, Sarah, ed. 2000. *Views from the South: The Effects of Globalization and the WTO on Third World Countries.* Oakland, CA: Food First Books.
Baiman, Ron, Heather Boushey, and Dawn Saunders, eds. 2000. "The Global Political Economy." In *Political Economy and Contemporary Capitalism,* Section V, 175–244. Armonk, NY: M.E. Sharpe.
Baker, Dean, Gerald Epstein, and Robert Pollin, eds. 1998. *Globalization and Progressive Economic Policy.* New York: Cambridge University Press.
Baran, Paul. 1957. *Political Economy of Growth.* New York: Monthly Review Press.

Barnet, Richard, and John Cavanagh. 1994. *Global Dreams: Imperial Corporations and the New World Order.* New York: Simon and Schuster.

Barnet, Richard, and Ronald Muller. 1974. *Global Reach: The Power of Multinational Corporations.* New York: Simon and Schuster.

Barone, Charles A. 1985. *Marxist Thought on Imperialism.* Armonk, NY: M.E. Sharpe.

Bello, Walden. 2001. *The Future in the Balance: Essays on Globalization and Resistance.* Oakland, CA: Food First Books.

Brecher, Jeremy, and Tim Costello. 1994. *Global Village or Global Pillage: Economic Reconstruction from the Bottom Up.* Boston: South End Press.

Coates, David. 2000. *Models of Capitalism.* Cambridge, MA: Polity Press.

DeMartino, George. 2000. *Global Economy, Global Justice, and Theoretical & Policy Alternatives to Neoliberalism.* New York: Routledge.

Frank, Andre Gunder. 1967. *Capitalism and Underdevelopment.* New York: Monthly Review Press.

Greider, William. 1997. *One World, Ready or Not: The Manic Logic of Global Capitalism.* New York: Simon and Schuster.

MacEwan, Arthur. 1999. *Neo-Liberalism or Democracy? Economic Strategy, Markets, and Alternatives for 21st Century.* New York: Zed Books.

Magdoff, Harry. 1978. *Imperialism: From the Colonial Age to the Present.* New York: Monthly Review Press.

Sherman, Howard. 1987. *Foundations of Radical Political Economy,* ch. 9. Armonk, NY: M.E. Sharpe.

"Special Issue: After Seattle: A New Internationalism." 2000. *Monthly Review* (July–August).

"Special Issue: Imperialism Now." 2003 *Monthly Review* (July–August).

Tabb, William K. 2001. *The Amoral Elephant: Globalization and the Struggle for Social Justice in the 21st Century.* New York: Monthly Review Press.

Wilber, C.K., ed. 1988. *The Political Economy of Development and Underdevelopment.* 4th ed. New York: Random House.

Yates, Michael D. 2003. *Naming the System: Inequality and Work in the Global Economy.* New York: Monthly Review Press.

Economic Crises

Baker, Dean, Gerald Epstein, and Robert Pollin, eds. 1998. *Globalization and Progressive Economic Policies.* New York: Cambridge University Press.

Bowles, Samuel, and Richard Edwards. 1993. *Understanding Capitalism.* New York: HarperCollins, chs. 13–16 and 18.

Brenner, Robert. 1998. "The Economics of Global Turbulence." *New Left Review* (May–June): 1–265.

Cherry, Robert et al., eds. 1987. *The Imperiled Economy. Book I: Macroeconomics from a Left Perspective.* Riverside, CA: Union for Radical Political Economics.

Crotty, James. 2000. "Structural Contradictions of the Global Neoliberal Regime." *Review of Radical Political Economics* 32, no. 3: 361–368.

Foster, John Bellamy, and Henryk Szlajfer, eds. 1984. *The Faltering Economy: The Problem of Accumulation Under Monopoly Capitalism.* New York: Monthly Review Press.

Goldstein, Jonathan P. 2000. "The Global Relevance of Marxian Crisis Theory." In *Political Economy and Contemporary Capitalism*, ed. Ron Baiman, Heather Boushey, and Dawn Saunders, 68–77. Armonk, NY: M.E. Sharpe.

Hossein-Zadeh, Ismael, and Anthony Gabb. 2000. "Long Waves of Capitalist Development and the Future of Capitalism." In *Political Economy and Contemporary Capitalism*, ed., Ron Baiman, Heather Boushey, and Dawn Saunders, 78–85. Armonk, NY: M.E. Sharpe.

Kotz, David, Terrence McDonough, and Michael Reich, eds. 1994. *Social Structures of Accumulation: The Political Economy of Growth and Crisis.* New York: Cambridge University Press.

Lippit, Victor. 1997. "The Reconstruction of a Social Structure of Accumulation in the U.S." *Review of Radical Political Economy* 20, no. 3: 11–21.

Magdoff, Harry, and Paul M. Sweezy. 1987. *Stagnation and the Financial Explosion.* New York: Monthly Review Press.

McDonough, Terrence. 1999. "Gordon's Accumulation Theory: The Highest Stage of Stadial Theory." *Review of Radical Political Economics* 31, no. 4: 6–31.

Michie, Jonathan, and John Grieve Smith, eds. 1999. *Global Instability and World Economic Governance.* New York: Routledge.

Moseley, Fred. 1999. "The United States Economy at the Turn of the Century: Entering a New Era of Prosperity?" *Capital and Class* (Spring): 25–45.

O'Hara, Philip Anthony. 2003. "Deep Recession and Financial Instability or a New Long Wave of Economic Growth for U.S. Capitalism? A Regulation School Approach." *Review of Radical Political Economics* 35: 18–43.

———. 2004. *A New Long Wave of Economics Growth for the U.S. Capitalism? A Social Structure of Accumulation and Regulation Analysis of Institutional and Technological Change.* New York: Routledge.

———. In press. "Recent Changes to the IMF, WTO and FSP: An Emerging Global Monetary-Trade-Production Social Structure of Accumulation for Long Wave Upswing." *Review of International Political Economy* 10, no. 3.

Sherman, Howard. 1987. *Foundations of Radical Political Economy.* Armonk, NY: M.E. Sharpe, chs. 6–7.

———. 1991. *The Business Cycle: Growth and Crisis Under Capitalism.* Princeton, NJ: Princeton University Press.

"Special Issue: Empirical Work in Marxian Crisis Theory." 1987. *Review of Radical Political Economics* 18, nos.1–2 (Spring–Summer).

Wolfson, Martin H. 1994. *Financial Crises: Understanding the Postwar U.S. Experience.* 2d ed. Armonk, NY: M.E. Sharpe.

6 RADICAL ALTERNATIVES TO CAPITALISM

When compared to what preceded it, capitalism has succeeded in producing rapid economic growth and has eliminated mass poverty, at least in the advanced industrialized capitalist countries like the United States. In this sense, radicals see capitalism as an economic system with many progressive qualities that has provided the material foundations for much of human progress over the last two centuries. Although capitalism can take much of the credit for this progress, in the radical perspective it must also share the blame for the very uneven spread of this progress and the mass poverty that persists in Third World countries like Brazil, India, and Nigeria.

When compared to the ideals of economic efficiency, quality of life, equity, and democracy, radical political economic analysis shows that capitalism seriously violates all four of these standards in ways that are fundamentally tied to the basic rules and organization of capitalism. This chapter begins with an evaluation of capitalism's performance from the radical perspective, followed by a discussion of alternatives to capitalism including existing socialist systems and the democratic socialist ideal favored by radical economists. The chapter will conclude with a discussion of capitalist reforms advocated by radicals. Although these reforms fall far short of democratic socialism, such reforms are seen as transformative, moving the United States along a path that might eventually lead to a democratic socialist society.

Capitalism's Performance

Economic Efficiency

In the radical perspective, capitalism is, despite its potential for economic growth, a highly inefficient system. Capitalist growth and profit depend upon keeping people's propensity to consume artificially high. Millions of dollars are spent each year by capitalists trying to convince consumers to spend their incomes on capitalist-produced goods and services, many of which radicals believe do little to satisfy real human needs. Rather than overcoming scarcity, capitalism thrives on perpetuating scarcity. It does so primarily through advertising, which destroys utility by making people feel dissatisfied with what they have at present. Style and model changes and planned obsolescence are all part of capitalist marketing strategies designed to keep consumption expenditures high. The resources used up by capitalist marketing efforts, as well as the dubious value of much of what is produced by capitalism, make it a very inefficient system in this view.

Perhaps the biggest waste in the United States, according to radicals, is the trillions of dollars worth of resources devoted to military over the last fifty years. Although such military spending protects capitalists' interests abroad in the face of the contradictions of global capitalism, and is a major source of profits for many large corporations that supply the military, in the RPE perspective such expenditures are largely unnecessary to the real defense and security needs of the United States (Center for Defense Information and Project on Defense Alternatives Web sites).

In agreement with economists from other perspectives, radicals cite the costs of externalities such as the destruction of the natural environment as inefficient. The rule of profitability forces capitalists (through competition) to take into account only those costs that they must pay for, imposing the costs of pollution on others who cannot charge capitalists for their discomfort, annoyance, and illness. This is certainly economically inefficient as well as unjust.

Another inefficiency emphasized by radicals is the failure of capitalism to fully utilize the labor force. Unemployment throughout the history of U.S. capitalism has, excluding the Great Depression, persistently been between 3 and 11 percent (Keyssar 1989) according to official government measures that understate the real level of unemployment by about a factor of two (Riddell et al. 2002). Earlier chapters have shown that radical economic analysis makes a strong case that unemployment is one of the major ways that capitalists in the United States maintain high rates of profit. Although the personal and human costs of unemployment are great, the cost to society in terms of lost output is quite large. Had there had been full employment in the United States during the years 1974 to 1993, $1.6 trillion worth of goods and services could have been produced that were not (Baumol and Blinder 2001, 506).

When we combine unemployment with the other costs caused by capitalist-generated business cycles and long-term economic crises, the failure of capitalism to use material and human resources efficiently is further compounded. Capitalists also misuse and waste human resources by keeping labor intensity high and by ignoring workers' health and safety on the job. In RPE, the capitalist rate of profit is, holding other factors constant, positively related to the pace of work. Therefore, it is in the capitalists' interest to maximize labor intensity, as well as avoid costly health and safety measures that would protect workers. Such abuses represent the failure of a capitalist system to conserve labor resources.

Although it is profitable in many instances for capitalists to discriminate, it is not efficient. An efficient economic system would allocate people, regardless of race or gender, in a way that fully utilized their productive capacities. It is quite clear that in the United States women in general and people of African, Asian, Latino, and Native American heritage are, when they are employed at all, underemployed in jobs that do not fully and efficiently utilize their skills and creative abilities.

In the RPE perspective then, the inner workings of capitalism generate outcomes that are highly inefficient and go well beyond the economic inefficiencies noted by neoclassical economists. A system that generates such waste cannot be called economically efficient.

Quality of Life

When it comes to the quality of life, capitalism does not fare much better in the radical analysis. The capitalist-imposed division of labor has created jobs that for the majority of workers are alienating: repetitive, boring, physically difficult, dangerous jobs that offer workers little sense of self-esteem or chance of developing their full human capabilities. Under capitalism workers are used as a means to enhance capitalist profits. However, workers must be evaluated not just as inputs in a production process, but also as products themselves. The fact that capitalism offers so few the chance for self-development and individual growth through challenging work condemns millions to lives of boredom and drudgery.

The many divisions placed between workers in the workplace isolates workers from each other, and capitalist labor markets force workers to compete with each other for employment and promotions. Such divisions and competition pose barriers to solidarity and prevent workers from developing meaningful relationships (both on and off the job) and developing their cooperative abilities. The stultification of human development caused by the capitalist division of labor and the barriers separating people impose serious limits to the quality of life under capitalism.

The dynamic nature of capitalism, while progressive in terms of economic growth, also generates forces that are inconsistent with the development of healthy family and community life. The intensity of labor and sometimes the long hours imposed on workers often leave them unable to participate fully in family life, enjoy leisure time, or to participate in community life. Unemployment disrupts family life for millions of families and the very low wages paid to large numbers of workers fall well below earnings that are adequate to meet the basic economic and social needs of healthy families. Indeed, poverty condemns whole communities in the United States to inadequate services and community life. The pursuit of life, liberty, and happiness depends upon having an adequate material base to do so.

The frequent interruption of capitalist economic growth by business cycles and recurrent long-term economic crises caused by the interworkings of the capital accumulation process are clearly not conducive to either family or community well-being. The mobility of capital since World War II has caused many plant closings that have left millions of workers and their communities without adequate income-producing opportunities necessary to sustain viable communities and healthy families. Capitalist labor markets have similar outcomes when, in order to gain promotions or better jobs, workers are compelled to move, leaving their relatives and communities behind. The average U.S. family moves once every six years (U.S. Bureau of the Census 2000).

Given the rules and organization of the capitalist economy, families and communities, like labor, are valued only when they generate sufficient profits for capitalists. The capitalist-organized labor process does not exist for the worker, the family, or the community. It exists solely for the profits of the owners of capital. This is the essence of capitalism. That capitalism does not provide a very high quality of life for millions people is perhaps understandable in this context.

Equality

When assessed against the value of equality, capitalism in the United States does very poorly. The distribution of income and wealth is so unequal that millions of people are left with low incomes that do not provide an adequate material basis for even a minimally decent life by U.S. standards as was shown in chapter 5. According to recent studies, almost one-third of families have income levels insufficient for basic family needs (Boushey et al. 2001). Such economic hardship, in the face of the opulence of the corporate wealthy, is in the radical view unjust. The extent of such inequality goes well beyond that necessary for incentive purposes. In fact, radicals argue that the enhanced productivity of the few with high incomes is in fact offset by the diminished productivity of the many whose low incomes offer little incentive to work hard (Best and Connolly 1982, ch. 2).

The tremendous income and wealth inequality in the United States is the result of the fact that the dominant capitalist class and, to a lesser extent, the middle classes are able to claim vastly disproportionate shares of the economic pie for themselves. They have the power to determine income shares based on their ownership of the means of production and position in the corporate hierarchical organization. Inheritance allows the transfer of wealth and privilege from one generation to the next, perpetuating inequality over time.

The subordinate working class has little economic power and must settle for small and in many cases inadequate shares of what they have produced with their labor. When it comes to public services (education, health, police, sanitation, and recreational services), working-class communities have far fewer services than middle-class and owning-class communities, and in many cases services are grossly inferior. In the radical perspective this is the result on the one hand of the economic exploitation inherent in U.S. capitalism and on the other the ability of the corporate wealthy to influence public (government) policy in their favor.

As unfair and unjust as insufficient incomes and inadequate public services are in general, they are even worse for ethnic and racial minorities and women because of capitalist discrimination. Given the rules and organization of capitalism, discrimination can enhance the position of capitalists in their competitive drive for profits. The growing gap between the incomes of white and black USers and the lack of significant economic progress for most women are evidence of both the degree and persistence of discrimination in U.S. capitalism despite the Civil Rights and Women's movements. Racial and gender economic equality are in this view incompatible with the capitalist organization of the labor process.

A fair and just economic system is one that shares both the benefits and burdens equitably. The capitalist assignment of burdens in the United States is, according to radicals, extremely unfair. The worst jobs are reserved first for racial minority men and women, then white women, and last for white working-class men. Unemployment is rarely experienced by the middle (although as we have seen this has been changed with corporate downsizing movement) and owning classes, and is concentrated among the same groups cited above. Black unemployment rates are twice the white rate, and worse for teenagers.

The benefits are equally unfair in their distribution. The belief that everyone has earned the income they receive has little to do with the actual basis for income distribution. The radical analysis of income distribution is much closer to the folk wisdom "them that has gits." In this view, power and position determine who gets what and this is rationalized on the basis of elitist (classist, racist, and sexist) ideologies that place a much lower value on the labor of working-class people, racial minorities, and women. It is not fair for managers to pay themselves the equivalent of $3,500 per hour when the average hourly wages of workers is about one-five hundredth of that amount and when several million workers work for a minimum wage that is insufficient for even a minimally decent life. It is not fair for nurses to be paid less than other comparable male professionals. It is not fair for the average black worker to make considerably less than white workers.

When examining inequality within the international capitalist system, the disparities are considerably more pronounced. While U.S., Japanese, and German multinational corporations have profited from their subsidiaries in the Third World, the people of the Third World have not benefited proportionally. Such exploitation has left in its wake extremely high rates of abject poverty, people living on the margins of biological subsistence. Malnutrition, disease, and high infant mortality are all too common in the Third World.

In the radical perspective these inequities are directly related to the basic structure of capitalism. Capitalism scores very low when it comes to fairness and equity. In addition to inequitable and un-fair distribution of burdens and benefits, both domestically and internationally, workers are generally mistreated on the job and denied full respect as human beings.

Democracy

Democracy is the fourth ideal standard against which to judge or evaluate the performance of capitalism. The idea of democracy is that the basic decisions affecting the lives of people should be considered and voted on by those who are affected. In the radical view, democracy as a principle can and should be applied to the economy and other social structures, as well as to the system of government. In the radical perspective, it is easy to see that the labor process and the family have their own governing systems, making the application of the democratic principle appropriate. All decisions, irrespective of the particular social sphere in which they occur, should be democratic, be it in the economy, family, or government.

One of the biggest contradictions of capitalism is between prop-erty rights and democratic rights. For example, the right of capi-talists to do as they wish with their property, such as close down a plant, clashes directly with the democratic principle of an individual's right to participate in decisions that affect their lives, in this case the rights of workers and affected community mem-bers. The capitalist control of the labor process in capitalism also clashes with the principle of democratic control of the labor pro-cess. In both of these cases, the property rights of capitalists su-persede the democratic rights of workers and the community. The owners and executives of the largest corporations have more day-to-day influence over the lives of people than elected gov-ernment officials.

In any social system we would want to know how capitalism promotes democratic governing principles. In the radical perspec-tive we have seen how the unequal distribution of income and wealth, control over the media and other idea-making institutions (education), and the one-class one-veto system work to seriously limit true democratic government decisions. Furthermore, the hierarchical nature of the capitalist-organized labor process does not promote democratic principles nor prepare people for democratic decision making. This further limits the effectiveness of U.S. democratic political institutions.

In an international context, democracy has fared much worse. Political and economic intervention in the Third World has been imperialistic, ignoring the sovereign democratic rights of these nations. Military intervention, CIA covert operations, as well as other policies, have been used to topple "unfriendly" governments and impose repressive dictatorial regimes supportive of foreign capitalist interests in many Third World countries. International organizations such as the World Bank, International Monetary Fund, and World Trade Organization promote and shield capitalist interests from democratic oversight. The spread of international terrorism to the United States from a radical perspective is the "blowback" created by decades of U.S. imperialistic policies (on "blowback," see www.zmag.org/sommerscalam.htm).

Even though patriarchy and racism predate capitalism, we have seen that capitalism has, in the radical view, perpetuated both to capitalist advantage. People of color have been denied the same access to democratic governing institutions as whites have had, even when one takes into account the limitations of capitalist democracy discussed above. The same holds true for all women regardless of race, who in addition are denied their basic democratic rights within their families due to the family patriarchical governing system.

We see then that there are serious limits to democracy in a capitalist system. Democracy is absent in the capitalist economy as well as in other social institutions such as the family. Political democracy, when it exists in capitalist countries (and it does not always), is limited in significant ways. Finally, on the international level imperialism not democracy is the norm for foreign relations between advanced industrialized capitalist countries and the Third World. In the radical view, workers, consumers, and citizens here and abroad should have a voice in the economic, social, and political decisions that affect their lives.

Conclusion

Significant deficiencies in the quality of life, equity, and democracy in capitalism compound the difficulty of attaining economic efficiency, which is already limited in other ways by capitalism. Unlike those who believe that there are trade-offs (e.g., more equality or democracy offset by less economic efficiency), radicals believe that within a broad range it is possible to have more efficiency, quality of life, equity, and democracy simultaneously. Radicals emphasize these positive relationships. When people are treated fairly, have healthy social lives, and have a voice in decisions that affect them, they work harder, are more cooperative and productive. This means that in capitalism the lack of quality of life, equity, and democracy all compound to retard economic efficiency.

However, radicals question the neoclassical practice of making economic efficiency primary over other evaluative criteria. Such beliefs may have more to do with the dominant ideology of capitalism that justifies a system that radicals believe cannot provide a high quality of life, fairness, or democracy, and is limited in its ability to provide even economic efficiency. On all counts capitalism falls considerably short of satisfying these fundamental human needs, even though capitalism represents an advance over previous economic systems.

Democratic Socialism

Capitalism is in the radical view fraught with defects: economic instability, perpetual unemployment for millions, militarism and imperialism, profound inequality and poverty in the face of plenty, deadening work and oppressive work conditions, perpetuation of racism and sexism, irrational materialism, environmental destruction, lack of democratic control of economic destiny, constraints on political democracy, and barriers to attainment of community, solidarity, and cooperation.

Given what are believed to be the systemic nature of these defects, correcting them requires, in the radical perspective, changing the rules and organization of the economic system, that is, replacing capitalism with some other way of organizing the labor process and system of production. Drawing on the ideas and principles set forth by Marx and extended by others, radical political economists advocate a democratic socialist system to replace capitalism. The radical vision of democratic socialism goes well beyond the ideas of Marx and well beyond currently existing and past forms of socialism. As such democratic socialism represents a contemporary vision for the future.

Although no blueprint exists for such a society, indeed it is probably beyond the realm of intellectual feasibility to blueprint any social system, radicals have outlined the principles on which such a society should be built and have in broad contour traced out what some of the basic democratic socialist institutions might look like. Such a society will be, radicals believe, more economically and socially efficient, fair and equitable, and democratic.

What is democratic socialism? To give one the flavor of the possible answers to this question, several advocates of democratic socialism in the United States will be quoted from "What Is Socialism?" (1985):

> Socialism is essentially a conservative idea. It involves establishing and maintaining purposes, qualities and institutions that nourish human life. It includes: (1) A sustainable relationship with the natural world; (2) Development of community, cooperation and concern for the dignity of all persons; (3) Creation of democracy in all aspects of living so that people have control over their own lives and provision for their basic needs; and (4) Construction of justice and peace in a complex world. (Robert Halbeisan)

> [Socialism is] A social doctrine and an economic system that basically opposes individualism and its concomitant exaggerated competitiveness, which makes wealth the one desirable goal, causes an excessive inequality of income, and exalts private ownership at the expense of the common good. Socialism advocates instead ownership and control of the means of production by the whole community with cooperation and fellowship as the desirable ends. (Blanche Jantzen)

The idea of socialism is that society can be organized to meet our most evident human needs, and that the key to such reorganization is democratic control of the economy. Democratic socialism—unlike other versions of "socialism"—is a system in which the internal organization and investment process of firms are controlled by democratic cooperatives. Though there are important exceptions to it, the principle characteristic of democratic socialism is that it seeks democratic control over society by the most decentralized means. (David O'Brien)

[Democratic socialism is] An economic system in which the means of production (productive property) are owned and democratically controlled by the community. Community is understood as a public or associative grouping more extensive than the extended family; it can vary from a nation state to a small voluntary cooperative as long as it is inclusive of all personnel. Socialism provides that as in political democracy every person shares in political power, so in economic democracy through shared control and ownership of productive property every person participates in economic power. The end is empowerment essential for minimal participation in the economic community as in the political community. (Stephen Charles Mott)

These statements give us a flavor of democratic socialism that is decidedly different than capitalism. The emphases on community, cooperation, equality, dignity for all, and individual freedom to take charge of one's destiny through shared systems of control, particularly of economic life, contrast sharply with capitalism, where control over the labor process and production is in the hands of a very small capitalist class, where community values are subordinated to corporate profitability, where competition is the order of the day for capitalists as well as the middle and working classes, where human dignity is denied to millions of people, and where poverty and tremendous inequalities persist.

How do radical economists propose to achieve their lofty goals? What kinds of changes do they propose?

Social Ownership

One of the proposals is a change in capitalism's key institution, private ownership of the means of production, the basis for capitalist power and control. Radicals advocate social ownership, replacing private ownership with social control of the means of production. Social control would be exercised through a combination of worker-owned and -managed enterprises and public enterprises.

A worker-managed firm would be owned by those who participate in the enterprise. The capital for public enterprises would come from government, which would make them state-owned. This does not mean necessarily that privately owned business would no longer exist, but it does mean that private ownership would be dramatically curtailed and limited to small businesses and farms, or family enterprises that do not rely significantly on outside labor.

Social control includes some combination of public control and worker control. Social control would mean that the community/ workers would control their own resources and labor processes, bringing production and distribution decisions under effective democratic control. For example, decisions concerning the size and use of the surplus product would be decided by the community/workers. At the end of the year the surplus would accrue to the community/workers and they would decide whether to reinvest it or to distribute it as increased consumption for some or all members of the community. Such increased consumption could the take the form of enhanced individual private consumption or public consumption, for example, providing day-care centers.

The surplus could be kept large or small depending upon the community/worker desire for publicly provided goods and economic growth. For example, a greater desire for such goods or economic growth would require greater surplus. Radicals believe that once people have democratic control over the labor process and resources, there will be less emphasis on materialism and thus less need for economic growth, a growing concern related to sustainable development. The proportion of total consumption made up of publicly provided goods will increase relative to private consumption goods. Under capitalism the provision of public goods is limited by capitalist resistance such as the effective resistance of the for-profit medical-industrial-insurance complex in the United

States to a public health-care system, despite the fact that millions of people in the United States have no medical insurance coverage and millions of others have inadequate coverage.

Socialist Enterprises

The predominate form of enterprise would be worker-owned and self-managed enterprises. Each worker would have an ownership share purchased if necessary with low-interest loans. Workers would own as well as participate in management. They would elect representatives to the enterprise board of directors. These representatives determine firm policies that would be carried out by a hired enterprise manager who in effect works for the workers. For many radicals the prototype for such enterprises is the extensive Mondragon producer cooperatives found in the Basque region of Spain. Established in 1956 the Mondragon cooperative complex has grown impressively into an $11 billion dollar enterprise with over 30,000 workers and annual sales of $5 billion in sales (Mondragon Web site; for a study see Whyte and Whyte 1991; and Gunn 2000). There is also a history of cooperative enterprise in the United States and although they are not extensive, many have been successful (Gunn 1984; Zwerdling 1980; for the benefits of greater participation see Blumberg 1969).

As democratic as such firms would be, there is no accountability mechanism to ensure that enterprises operate in the public interest. It would be unrealistic to assume that the interests of an enterprise's workers would always coincide with the general public interest. One way to deal with this would be to have public representatives on the boards of all enterprises to represent the interests of the public, such as consumer and environmental interests.

In addition to worker-managed firms, there would be public enterprises owned by federal, state, or local governments. However, these firms would also be set up along the lines of worker-managed enterprises and would be required to have worker representatives on their management boards. Public enterprises would exist in cases of natural monopolies such as utilities as well as in crucial industries such as transportation, telecommunications, health care, and banking.

Clearly these socialist enterprises would overcome several of the defects of capitalist-organized production where workers and the public have little to no voice in corporate decision making. Democracy would prevail in socialist enterprises, and it would be expected that the harsh treatment of workers under capitalism would cease. In the absence of private property in the means of production, people would be unable to amass great wealth and, therefore, equality would be greatly enhanced. Additionally, the distribution of income between unskilled and skilled workers and professionals would more than likely be more egalitarian given democratic control over wage and salary decisions.

The result would be a more equal and fair distribution of both the benefits and burdens of the economy. Democratic control would ensure that workers were not treated as mere inputs or a means to someone else's ends. Workers directly affected by technological changes would have a voice in the decisions over appropriate technology that enhanced both labor productivity and work satisfaction.

Although it might be thought that these goals are in conflict, radicals believe that enhancing work satisfaction also enhances labor productivity. Democratizing the labor process and the process of production should unleash a tremendous amount of socialist productivity that would be impossible to achieve within the capitalist-dominated labor process. Under capitalism these two goals are frequently in conflict because enhancing work satisfaction usually means giving workers greater control over the labor process, something capitalists are unwilling to relinquish given the competitive pressures to maximize profits discussed in chapter 3.

It should be emphasized that the radical emphasis here is on structures rather than specific outcomes. Although conflicts are bound to exist in socialism, providing democratic structures that guarantee people involvement in decision making means that disputes and conflicts between people and different groups of people will be mediated democratically in all spheres of society.

Planning Versus Markets

Beyond the ownership and structure of enterprise, what mechanism do radicals advocate for coordinating decision making among firms? In capitalism markets are the primary regulating mechanism supplemented by very limited government regulation, at least in the United States. Although no government planning takes place, a substantial amount of planning takes place within corporations that have acquired subsidiaries through horizontal, vertical, and conglomerate mergers. In these cases firms that were previously coordinated through the market are the subject of intrafirm corporate planning.

There has been substantial debate among radicals over planning versus markets. Advocates of planning have been criticized because of the failures of centralized planning in countries like the Soviet Union before its breakup. Such planning required a large bureaucracy that gave planners a great deal of power. Such a bureaucratic and perhaps monolithic central planning apparatus would offset the decentralized democratic gains of employee-run enterprises.

Some radical economists have counterpoised to central planning a vision of decentralized democratic planning that relies on the elected representatives of enterprises and communities who would come together to determine a plan that coordinated their activities (Gunn 2000; Mandel 1986; Albert and Hahnel 1983). Although such bottom-up planning may be theoretically feasible, the planning process would require a great deal of time spent in meetings to come up with a plan that everyone could live with and that would coordinate the production plans of individual enterprises. It is unlikely in a complex industrial economy that such a planning process would be desirable let alone very efficient.

Using the market to coordinate socialist enterprises might seem the only feasible solution. However, market socialism has had its

own difficulties. Before the breakup of Yugoslavia, market socialism exhibited some of the same tendencies that plague market
capitalism: uneven development, monopoly, inflation, cyclical
unemployment, and income disparities between firms. Therefore,
the market solution is not without its own attendant difficulties.

Combining Planning and Markets

If planning is flawed and markets are flawed what is left? Many
radicals advocate a mixed system of coordination that takes advantage of the benefits of markets while offsetting their defects
with government planning and regulation. Markets are a wonder-
fully decentralized mechanism for coordinating, through supply
and demand, the decisions of enterprises. Markets ensure enterprise discipline and efficiency through competition, rewarding
enterprises according to their performance in the marketplace.

With a more egalitarian distribution of income, socialist markets would be much more efficient at registering the needs of consumers. In capitalism, many of the needs of the poor and those
with low incomes go unmet while the very rich and wealthy command a standard of living that, according to radicals, is grossly
excessive. Under democratic socialism, the range of publicly provided free goods would be extended (e.g., health care, transportation, adequate housing, day care, community art/recreation centers,
etc.). Distribution of these goods would be distributed on the basis
of citizen rights, rather than market-based criteria.

As the experience with market capitalism shows, market outcomes are not always in the social interest. Unemployment, environmental destruction, economically depressed communities and
regions, and monopoly are all market-generated problems. Therefore, where markets are inadequate, they must be modified by priorities established by a planning process at local, state, and federal
levels. Planning priorities would be established through a democratic political process that would establish production and investment goals. Market criteria for success and failure would be
supplemented with social criteria.

The availability of resources would be determined by the division of surplus between socialist enterprises (for reinvestment and enhanced private consumption) and local, state, and national government (for public investment and consumption). This division of the surplus, through taxes, is one way in which market outcomes would be modified. For example, tax subsidies could be given to an enterprise where based on market criteria alone expansion was unwarranted, but the benefits to the community warranted expanded production. Of course, more successful enterprises would still have to be left with sufficient surplus to reward their superior performance in the market.

Discovering the real social costs of all planning proposals would be of primary importance in making rational choices. Public debates would take place over priorities and would be resolved by an enhanced socialist democratic structure that guaranteed more effective political participation and representation of different groups and interests than exist at present in democratic capitalist governments. The absence of a corporate capitalist class would eliminate that class's one-class one-veto control over the political process. The decentralized democratic control of socialist enterprises would minimize the possibility for any one group gaining similar influence over government decision making (for discussion of such democratic structures see Gintis 1983).

Planning would ensure that the benefits of worker-managed enterprise productivity be shared to some degree with the larger society, but without discouraging enterprise initiative. A certain proportion of the surplus would accrue to local, state, and national governments, as discussed above. Such funds would be used to finance government operations, the provision of public goods, welfare for those unable to work, as well as form a pool of government investment resources. The latter could be loaned out to fund new worker-managed or public enterprises or used to subsidize existing enterprises when it is socially desirable to do so.

Primary to the planning process would be some government control over investment priorities so that investment can be channeled into those areas that meet social priorities, such as health care, education, housing, and economic development of depressed communities/regions. In this way, government modifies market-established priorities, bringing them in line with social priorities. Unmet social needs can be met by government-established incentives or directly by public (local, state, or national) investment.

The public would in this way also have control over employment levels and the allocation of labor, supplementing the demand for labor when market demand is insufficient to maintain full employment. Under democratic socialism everyone who wanted a job would be guaranteed a job, if necessary in the public sector. Unlike U.S. capitalism, unemployment would not have to be resorted to under democratic socialism to maintain control over labor and thus maximize profits.

In order to ensure social priorities, radicals propose that many crucial industries such as steel or banking and natural monopolies such as utilities be nationalized. Public enterprises would be subject to the same rules of democratic decision making as worker-managed enterprises and subject to the same efficiency criteria as market-based enterprises. Government-owned enterprises give government control over the commanding heights of the socialist economy, further enabling it to ensure some degree of democratic established social priorities within the context of a market-based worker-managed socialist enterprise economy. The exact mix of enterprises would, like the mix of market and plan, have to be worked out in practice.

Government under socialism would continue to control the macroeconomy through fiscal-monetary growth and stabilization policies. Government would also regulate worker-managed enterprises to ensure that they operate in the social interest. Regulations concerning the environment, market behavior, employment practices, discrimination, consumer product safety, and so on, would emanate from government and be enforced by some combination of government regulating bodies and public representatives on enterprise boards of directors.

Government would also through the democratic political process regulate income distribution by establishing an income floor and ceiling beyond which wages/salaries could not fall or rise. Within this range enterprises would be able to set their own levels of labor remuneration depending upon productivity and democratic consensus within individual enterprises. The result would be a socially desirable income distribution. The specific degree of equality (or inequality) depends upon the specific consensus reached, but would in the radical view be much more egalitarian than at present under capitalism.

In the words of democratic socialist Michael Harrington (1989, 70), "within the context of a plan, markets could be, for the first time, an instrument for truly maximizing the freedom of choice of individuals and communities . . . the visible hand can use the invisible hand for its own purposes."

Gender and Racial Equality

Central to the democratic socialist transformation of society in the radical perspectives is the liberation of women and people of color. With economic structures that emphasize cooperation and solidarity, and with full employment, the economic environment will be more conducive to racial and gender equality.

However, a democratic socialist economic transformation will not in and of itself eliminate gender and racial discrimination. Given the persistence of racism and sexism for many centuries, and given the way it has been embedded in social institutions and culture, eliminating prejudice and discrimination will require concerted efforts and strong political leadership. Therefore, radicals make eliminating racism and sexism one of their top social priorities for a democratic socialist society.

This will require massive government and educational efforts to prevent discrimination and develop programs to advance women and people of color to the same level as white males. There would be free day-care programs, promotion of equal male responsibility for child care and domestic labor, and free education and training programs for those who have been denied the equal opportunity to develop their skills and creative abilities. There would also be allocation of resources for community development to make livable communities in urban racial ghettos and poor rural communities so that people will have access to jobs, adequate housing, health care, community services, schools, and cultural institutions.

Only with such massive efforts will racial and gender equality become a reality in democratic socialism. Although theoretically possible under capitalism, the capitalist rules and organization of the labor process mitigate against such an outcome as long as discrimination is profitable for capitalists and as long as people are forced to compete for scarce job opportunities. Democratic socialism offers an economic structure more conducive to solidarity and cooperation, even though that structure by itself will not guarantee gender and racial equality. Only by making racial and gender equality a top social priority in democratic socialism will such an outcome be possible (for a provocative discussion on race and socialism see Marable 1983).

International Relations

The imperialism of capitalism would be superseded under democratic socialism. There would be no ownership of enterprises in other countries, removing one of the major reasons for an imperialistic foreign policy under capitalism. The capitalist ideology of free trade and practice of protectionist beggar-thy-neighbor policies would be replaced with a democratic socialist policy of managed trade, bringing planning to international markets.

The goal of international democratic socialist planning would be the same as domestic planning, to coordinate international economic transactions in a way that meets both national interests and the interests of the rest of the world. This will require some kind of international governing body, perhaps with elected representatives from each country. Although difficult to imagine at this point in our history, clearly such a democratic governing body is essential to achieving a peaceful and just world order within which all peoples can flourish.

Given the emphasis on democracy, cooperation, and solidarity in democratic socialism, radicals advocate foreign policies based on demilitarization and world peace. Economic aid to underdeveloped Third World countries would be a high priority. Such aid would be directed immediately toward ending hunger in the short term and toward the long-term objective of helping Third World countries become self-sufficient where possible in the production of basic human needs such as food, clothing, shelter, and other basic necessities.

Conclusion

The alternative to capitalism proposed by radicals is decidedly different. Democratic socialism is designed to overcome the deficiencies of capitalism by bringing the labor process, production, and distribution under social and democratic control through worker-managed and public enterprises, markets supplemented by government planning, an enhanced democratic political process, concerted efforts to end discrimination against women and people of color, and a foreign policy of peace and social justice for all people. Such changes would, in the radical view, bring substantial gains in economic efficiency, quality of life, equity, and democracy.

Existing Socialism

What do radicals have to say about countries that claim or have claimed to be socialist such as the Soviet Union, China, Yugoslavia, or Cuba? Although a thorough treatment of this topic is outside the scope of this chapter, the basic radical analysis of existing socialism will be briefly summarized here. The radical analytical approach to the study of these "socialist" societies is the same three-dimensional approach used above to study capitalist societies, and they are evaluated using radical ideals of democratic socialism.

In most cases, radicals are very critical of these societies because they do not conform to the democratic socialist ideal proposed above.

Although such countries are to be applauded for their noble efforts to build socialist societies, in practice many of these socialist experiments have not lived up to their expectations. In part, radicals explain these failures by the very backward nature of these countries, their extreme poverty, and lack of democratic traditions when socialism was initiated. Therefore, the socialist vision and practice in these countries has fallen considerably short of the democratic socialism advocated by radicals, a vision designed not for a poor underdeveloped country, but for an advanced industrial society.

In the case of the Soviet Union, the Soviet economy and society, despite the absence of a capitalist class, was a class-dominated system in many ways more oppressive than capitalism, at least when compared to those countries where capitalism is joined with political democracy. Many of the repressive characteristics of the Soviet Union were shared with countries like South Korea, Chile, and the Philippines, where capitalism was joined with political dictatorship. The Soviets lacked democracy, both political and economic. Their highly centralized planning structures were both undemocratic and inefficient, particularly in the more advanced stages of industrialization. In this stage of development centralized coordination becomes quite difficult given the complexity of the economy and the large amount of information needed to make rational economic decisions.

Radicals refer to such "socialist" societies as state bureaucratic socialism or the statist mode of production. State ownership of the means of production gives power and control in such societies to a state bureaucratic and party elite that dominates the government, central planning organs, and enterprise management. This elite group functions as a ruling class controlling both economic and political decision making. Such control gives them command over the economic surplus, its division, and the labor process.

Workers in the Soviet Union worked under hierarchical conditions not too different from workers under capitalism. One difference is that unions were run by the state and did not represent worker interests within the enterprise. Wages were set essentially by labor supply and full employment placed workers in a relatively advantageous situation. Nonetheless, workers had less income and fewer privileges than managers and state and party elites, and worked under conditions little different from workers in the United States. They did not have control over their own labor process and were alienated from the decision-making process.

On the positive side, income distribution was, despite the inequalities noted above, more egalitarian; full employment was guaranteed; and a much broader range of social services was subsidized or provided free than found in industrialized capitalist countries. The Soviets were able to develop in a short period of time basic industry, an advanced educational system, and basic health care. Additionally, they were able to match the United States militarily and had a well- developed space program. Such successes compare favorably with capitalism, particularly when similar stages of development are compared and when compared to the capitalist experience in many Third World countries.

However, the quality of goods and services was poor, economic growth during the post-1960 period was weak, and the overall standard of living low compared to advanced industrial capitalist countries. The Cold War drain on Soviet resources contributed to economic difficulties. When coupled with the lack of basic human rights and political freedoms taken for granted in capitalist countries such as the United States, countries like the Soviet Union do not offer an attractive alternative to capitalism.

A socialist country that is more consistent with the kind of democratic socialism proposed by radicals was Yugoslavia. There enterprises were worker-managed but markets were the predominate form of enterprise coordination. Like the Soviet Union, Yugoslavia had an impressive record of economic development until the 1980s when its growth stalled. The governing body in Yugoslavia was a one-party state that, while less repressive than the Soviet Union, still fell short of meeting the standards of U.S. democracy, not to mention the yet higher standards of the enhanced democratic state sought by democratic socialists. The major radical criticism of Yugoslav market socialism was that the market-based coordination of worker-managed enterprises produced the socially undesirable outcomes of unemployment, instability, inflation, monopoly, and income inequality between workers of different enterprises. In fact, overreliance on the market has, according to radicals, led to a decline of workers' management and greater emphasis on the decisions of professionals and managers. The regional income inequality and uneven development fostered by the market mechanism fueled the historic ethnic and religious conflicts within Yugoslavia, which contributed to the collapse of market socialism in the 1980s.

The failure of some of the existing socialisms to produce viable systems consistent with the current needs of their people led in the late 1980s to dramatic reform movements in country after country and the collapse of "socialism" in the Soviet Union and Eastern European countries. The current trend has not been toward democratizing socialism, but rather toward democratic market capitalism, particularly in the countries of Eastern Europe and the countries that made up the old Soviet Union. At the time of their collapse, radical economists were generally quite pessimistic about the prospects of successful transitions to market-based capitalism, and, after more than a decade of capitalist reforms, success in these countries has been quite limited and in some cases economic and social conditions are worse than before.

While capitalism has been successful in some parts of the world (e.g., Western Europe, North America, Japan), radicals point out that it has failed in many if not most places it has been tried (Third World countries, for example). Capitalist reforms in what used to be "socialist" countries are likened by radicals to Third World attempts to develop industrial capitalism, which have in the vast majority of cases failed, in part due to imperial domination and exploitation by the advanced capitalist countries. The solution in these countries is not capitalism, according to radicals, but rather a mixed system of democratic socialism like that proposed for the United States by radical economists.

The economic problem facing those societies from a socialist point of view was "combining democratic central planning of the volume of new investment with decentralized, market control of day-to-day production" (Sherman 1990). China has been trying to introduce markets and some degree of private enterprise within an overall planned system and it may end up following the capitalist road rather than a democratic socialist road. China's attempt to "liberalize" its economy has produced noteworthy successes in terms of economic growth, but at a cost of greater inequality and hardship imposed on Chinese workers.

Likewise Cuba, in the face an economic crisis caused by the collapse of the Soviet Union and the devastating loss of its sugar market, has had to introduce economic institutional reforms including the limited introduction of private enterprise and limited use of markets. Unlike China, Cuba has been much more cautious about reforming Cuban socialism in ways that it sees as consistent with socialist principles and goals, and as a result Cuban socialism is viewed much more favorably by radical economists. Cuban success in education, health care, and provision of families' basic economic needs, as well as the Cuban commitment to socialist principles, has been viewed by radicals as an alternative model of economic and social development for those countries that make up the underdeveloped capitalist world.

Reforming Capitalism

Most radicals believe that democratic socialism is not currently feasible in the United States and probably will not be politically feasible for some time to come. Even if it were on the political agenda, the transition from capitalism to democratic socialism presents complex difficulties. Many radicals argue that to successfully achieve democratic socialism the means must be democratic and peaceful, rather than forceful and violent. This is certainly one lesson that can be learned from the experience of existing socialist countries that have quite often relied on force and violence to gain people's cooperation. Clearly this is inconsistent with the values and norms that characterize the radical democratic socialist vision, and although force and violence are reprehensible, they should be viewed in the historical context. On this score even capitalism in its early stages fares pretty poorly.

In the minds of some radicals, change, even revolutionary changes such as those advocated by democratic socialism, should be evolutionary (Boggs and Boggs 1974). Given the political reality in most capitalist countries, the best that these radicals can hope for is reforming capitalism in ways that might someday be transformative, that is, reforms that might lead to a democratic socialist society. It is this hope that lies behind the reform proposals advocated by radicals. One way to view radical reforms is by using the radical concept of the social structure of accumulation (SSA), that is, the laws, institutions, and social customs that structure and regulate domestic and international relations among capitalists, between capitalists and workers, among workers, and between government and the economy. (This concept was discussed earlier in chapters 2 and 5).

Radical reforms can be viewed as a set of proposals that articulate a new U.S. social structure of accumulation that is decidedly democratic and pro-worker. Such reforms are often referred to as "Economic Democracy" a label we will adopt for this new SSA. Table 6.1 lists a set of democratic rights advocated by radicals for the United States.

Although these proposed democratic rights are radical in nature, the institutional changes necessary to implement these rights are within the framework of an essentially capitalist-organized economy. Although space does not permit a discussion of the specifics of these reforms, what all of these reforms have in common is that they mediate the social conflict between workers and citizens on the one hand, and capitalists on the other hand, in ways that generate more cooperation and less competition. The economic democracy social structure of accumulation will channel people's productive energies away from conflicting disputes and toward more economically and socially productive activities (For more complete discussion see Bowles et al. 1985, chs. 12–16; Carnoy and Shearer 1980; and Alperovitz and Faux 1984).

With an SSA that emphasizes economic democracy, gains in economic and social efficiency, fairness, and democracy will be

---

Table 6.1

Radical Democratic Rights

I. Right to economic security and equity
    1. Right to a decent job
    2. Solidarity wages, comparable pay, and equal employment opportunity
    3. Public child care and community service centers
    4.'A shorter standard work week and flexible work hours
    5. Flexible price controls
II. Right to a democratic workplace
    6. Public commitment to democratic trade unions
    7. Worker's right to know and decide
    8. Democratic productive incentives
    9. Promoting community enterprises
III. Right to chart our economic futures
    10. Planning to meet human needs
    11. Democratizing investment
    12. Democratic control of money supply
    13. Promoting community life
    14. Environmental democracy
    15. Democratizing foreign trade
IV. Right to better way of life
    16. Reduced military spending
    17. Conservation and safe energy
    18. Good food
    19. A national health policy
    20. Lifetime learning and cultural opportunities
    21. Payment for home child care in single-parent households
    22. Community corrections and reduced crime-control spending
    23. Community needs information and reduced advertising expenditures
    24. Equitable taxation and public allocation of resources

Source: From Samuel Bowles et al., *Beyond the Wasteland* (Garden City, NY: Anchor, 1984), 270. Reprinted with permission.

---

sufficient to benefit workers and citizens, as well as capitalists. The end result, according to radicals, will be to reform contemporary capitalism in ways that allow all boats to be lifted by the rising tide of capitalist growth rather the current growing divide between capitalists and everyone else.

How do radicals think such proposals will become a reality? They believe that such proposals will be popular with the vast majority of working people and could provide the basis for a greatly expanded labor movement that in coalition with other progressive groups—such as women, minorities, and environmentalists—could spearhead a social and political movement sufficient to pass and

implement economic democratic reforms. Many radical economists work with these progressive groups in the hopes that their
ideas will take root and help to spark the necessary social and
political movements (see listing of such groups in the further reading section at the end of this chapter).

Should radical reforms become an economic and political reality, and there are no indications at present that they will, their transformative potential is obvious provided the reforms are successful.
Such evolutionary changes allow experimentation with some elements of democratic socialism, without the need for revolutionary
change in the basic capitalist organization of production.

References

Albert, Michael, and Robin Hahnel. 1983. "Participatory Planning." In *Socialist
Visions*, ed. Steve Rosskamm Shalom, 247–274. Boston: South End Press.

Alperovitz, Gar, and Jeff Faux. 1984. *Rebuilding America: A Blueprint for the
New Economy.* New York: Pantheon.

Baumol, William J., and Alan S. Blinder. 2001. *Economics: Principles and Policies.* 8th ed. New York: Harcourt, Brace, Jovanovich.

Best, Michael, and William E. Connolly. 1982. *The Politicized Economy.* 2d ed.
Lexington, MA: D.C. Heath.

Blumberg, Paul. 1969. *Industrial Democracy: The Sociology of Participation.*
New York: Schocken Books.

Boggs, James, and Grace Boggs. 1974. *Revolution and Evolution in the Twentieth Century.* New York: Monthly Review Press.

Boushey, Heather et al. 2001. *Hardships in America. The Real Story of Working
Families.* Washington, DC: Economic Policy Institute.

Bowles, Samuel, David M. Gordon, and Thomas E. Weisskopf. 1984. *Beyond
the Wasteland: A Democratic Alternative to Economic Decline.* Garden City,
NY: Anchor Books.

Carnoy, Martin, and Derek Shearer. 1980. *Economic Democracy.* Armonk, NY:
M.E. Sharpe.

Center for Defense Information: www.cdi.org.

Gintis, Herb. 1983. "A Socialist Democracy for the United States: Representation and Participation." In *Socialist Visions*, ed. Steve Rosskamm Shalom,
11–55. Boston: South End Press.

Gunn, Christopher. 1984. *Workers' Self-Management in the United States.* Ithaca,
NY: ILR Press.

———. 2000. "Markets Against Economics Democracy." *Review of Radical
Political Economics* (September): 448.

Harrington, Michael. 1989. "Markets and Plans: Is the Market Necessarily Capitalist?" *Dissent* (Winter): 70.

Keyssar, Alexander. 1989. "History and the Problem of Unemployment." *Socialist Review* 4: 15–34.

Mandel, Ernest. 1986. "A Critique of Market Socialism." *New Left Review* 159 (September–October): 5–38.

Marable, Manning. 1983. "The Third Reconstruction: Black Nationalism and Race Relations After the Revolution." In *Socialist Visions*, ed. Steve Rosskamm, 101–127. Boston: South End Press.

Mondragon Corporacion Cooperativa Web site: www.mondragon.es/english/mcc.

The Project on Defense Alternatives: www.comw.org/pda.

Riddell, Tom et al. 2002. *Economics: A Tool for Critically Understanding Society*, 6th ed. Reading, MA: Addison-Wesley.

Shalom, Steve Rosskamm, ed. 1983. *Socialist Visions*. Boston: South End Press.

Sherman, Howard J. 1990. "The Second Soviet Revolution or the Transition from Statism to Socialism." *Monthly Review* (March): 21.

U.S. Bureau of the Census. 2001 *Current Population Reports, Geographical Mobility: March 1999 to March 2000, Population Characteristics*, Series P-20, No. 538 (May 2001), Table A.

"What Is Socialism?" 1985. *Religious Socialism* (Spring). Published by the Religion and Socialism Commission of the Democratic Socialists of America.

Whyte, William, and Kathleen Whyte. 1991. *Making Mondragon*. Ithaca, NY: Cornell University Press.

Zwerdling, Daniel. 1980. *Workplace Democracy: A Guide to Workplace Ownership, Participation, and Self-Management Experiments in the United States and Europe*. New York: Colophon Books.

Further Reading

Evaluating Capitalism

Albelda, Randy, and Chris Tilly. 1997. *Glass Ceilings and Bottomless Pits: Women's Work, Women's Poverty*. Boston: South End Press.

Blau, Joel. 1999. *Illusions of Prosperity: America's Working Families in an Age of Economic Insecurity*. New York: Oxford University Press.

Bowles, Samuel, and Richard Edwards. 1985. *Understanding Capitalism*. New York: Harper and Row, ch. 15.

Brouwer, Steve. 1998. *Sharing the Pie: A Citizens Guide to Wealth and Power in America*. New York: Henry Holt.

Collins, Chuck, and Felice Yeskel. 2000. *Economic Apartheid in America*. New York: Free Press.

Freeman, Harold. 1979. *Toward Socialism in America*. Part I. Cambridge, MA: Schenkman.

Heintz, James, and Nancy Folbre. 2000. *The Ultimate Field Guide to the U.S. Economy: A Compact and Irreverent Guide to Economic Life in America*. New York: The New Press.

Mészáros, István. 2001. *Socialism or Barbarism: From the "American Century" to the Cross Roads*. New York: Monthly Review Press.

Mishel, Lawrence, Jared Bernstein, and Heather Boushey. 2003. *The State of Working America 2002/2003*. Ithaca, NY: Cornell University Press.

Schweickart, David. 1996. *Against Capitalism*. Boulder, CO: Westview Press.

Sklar, Holly. 1995. *Chaos or Community? Seeking Solutions, Not Scapegoats for Bad Economics*. Boston: South End Press.

Zweig, Michael. 2000. *The Working Class Majority: America's Best Kept Secret*. Ithaca, NY: Cornell University Press.

Democratic Socialism

Albert, Michael, and Robin Hahnel. 1982. *Socialism Today and Tomorrow*. Part III. Boston: South End Press.

———. 1990. *The Political Economy of Participatory Economics*. Princeton, NJ: Princeton University Press.

Bowles, Samuel, and Herbert Gintis, eds. 2000. *Recasting Egalitarianism: New Rule For Communities, States, and Markets*. New York: Verso.

Busky, Donald. 2000. *Democratic Socialism: A Global Survey*. Westport, CT: Praeger.

Cullenberg, Steve. 1992. "Socialism's Burden: Toward a 'Thin' Definition of Socialism." *Rethinking Marxism* 5 (Summer): 64–83.

Edwards, Richard et al., eds. 1986. *The Capitalist System*. 3d ed. Englewood Cliffs, NJ: Prentice-Hall, ch. 11.

Einstein, Albert. [1949] 2000. "Why Socialism?" *Monthly Review* (May).

Freeman, Harold. 1979. *Towards Socialism in America. Part II*. Cambridge, MA: Schenkman.

Gunn, Christopher. 2000. "Markets Against Economic Democracy." *Review of Radical Political Economics* 32, no. 3 (September): 448–460.

Harrington, Michael. 1989. "Markets and Plans: Is the Market Necessarily Capitalist?" *Dissent* (Winter): 56–70.

Horvat, Branko. 1982. *The Political Economy of Socialism*. Armonk, NY: M.E. Sharpe.

Howard, Michael. 2000. *Self Management and the Crisis of Socialism: The Rose in the Fist of the Present*. Lanham, MD: Rowman and Littlefield.

Mandel, Ernest. 1986. "A Critique of Market Socialism." *New Left Review* 159 (September–October): 5–38.

Matthaei, Julie. 2000. "Beyond Racist Capitalist Economics: Growing a Liberated Economy." In *Political Economy and Contemporary Capitalism*, ed. Ron Baiman, Heather Boushey, and Dawn Saunders, 48–56. Armonk, NY: M.E. Sharpe.

Nove, Alec. 1983. *The Economics of Feasible Socialism*. London: Allen and Unwin.

Ollman, Bertell, ed. 1998. *Market Socialism: The Debate Among Socialists*. New York: Routledge.

Panitch, Leo, and Colin Leys, eds. 2000. *Necessary and Unnecessary Utopias: Socialist Register 2000*. New York: Monthly Review Press.

Roemer, John. 1994. *A Future for Socialism*. Cambridge, MA: Harvard University Press.

Ruccio, David. 1992. "Failure of Socialism, Future of Socialists?" *Rethinking Marxism* 5 (Summer): 7–22.

Schweickart, David. 1996. *Against Capitalism*. Boulder CO: Westview Press.

Shalom, Steve Rosskamm, ed. 1983. *Socialist Visions*. Boston: South End Press.

Sherman, Howard. 1987. *Foundations of Radical Political Economy*. Armonk, NY: M.E. Sharpe, 1987, ch. 17.

Weisskopf, Thomas. 1992. "Toward a Socialism for the Future, in the Wake of the Demise of the Socialism of the Past." *Review of Radical Political Economics* 24 (Fall and Winter): 1–28.

Existing Socialism and Failed Attempts

Cuba

Albert, Michael, and Robin Hahnel. 1981. *Socialism Today and Tomorrow*. Boston: South End Press, ch. 4.

Azicri, Max. 2000. *Cuba Today and Tomorrow: Reinventing Socialism*. Miami: University Press of Florida.

Campbell, Al. 1997. "Cuba Today and the Future of Cuban Socialism." *Monthly Review* (March): 21–32.

Fitzgerald, Frank T. 1994. *The Cuban Revolution in Crisis: From Managing Socialism to Managing Survival*. New York: Monthly Review Press.

Koont, Sinan. 1994. "Cuba: An Island Against All Odds." *Monthly Review* (October): 1–18.

MacDonald, Theodore. 1995. *Hippocrates in Havana: Cuba's Health Care System*. Mexico City: Bolivar Books.

MacEwan, Arthur. 1981. *Revolution and Economic Development in Cuba*. New York: St. Martin's Press.

Prada, Pedro. 1995. *Island Under Siege: The U.S. Blockade of Cuba*. Melbourne, Australia: Ocean Press.

Rosset, Peter, and Medea Benjamin, eds. 1994. *The Greening of the Revolution: Cuba's Experiment with Organic Agriculture*. Melbourne, Australia: Ocean Press.

Schwab, Peter. 1997. "Cuban Health Care and the U.S. Embargo." *Monthly Review* (November):15–26.

Sobrino, Francisco. 2001. "Socialism, Democracy, and Cuba." *Against the Current* (September/October): 30–34.

Stubbs, Jean. 1989. *Cuba the Test of Time*. New York: Latin American Bureau-Monthly Review Press.

Zimbalist, Andrew, and Claus Brundenius. 1990. *The Cuban Economy: Measurement and Analysis of Socialist Performance*. Baltimore: Johns Hopkins University Press.

Zimbalist, Andrew, Howard Sherman, and Stuart Brown. 1989. *Comparing Economic Systems: A Political Economic Approach*. 2d ed. New York: Harcourt Brace Jovanovich, ch. 12.

Soviet Union

Albert, Michael, and Robin Hahnel. 1981. *Socialism Today and Tomorrow.* Boston: South End Press, ch. 2.

Bilenkin, Vladimir. 1996. "Russian Workers Under Yeltsin's Regime: Notes on a Class in Defeat." *Monthly Review* (November): 1–11.

Deutscher, Issac. 1967. *The Unfinished Revolution.* New York: Oxford University Press.

Holmstrom, Nancy, and Richard Smith. 2000. "The Necessity of Gangster Capitalism: Primitive Accumulation in Russia and China." *Monthly Review* (February): 1–15.

Kagarlitsky, Boris. 1990. *Dialectics of Change.* New York: Verso.

———. 1995. *Restoration in Russia: Why Capitalism Failed.* New York: Verso.

Kotz, David. 1997. *Revolution from Above: The Demise of the Soviet System.* New York: Routledge.

Mandel, Ernest. 1989. *Beyond Perestroika.* New York: Verso.

Menshikov, Stanislav. 1999. "Russian Capitalism Today." *Monthly Review* (July/August): 81–99.

Miliband, Ralph, and Leo Panitch, eds. 1991. *Socialist Register 1991: Communist Regimes: The Aftermath.* New York: Monthly Review Press.

Sheppard, Barry. 2001. "Lessons of History and Theory: Theories of the USSR Following Its Collapse." *Against the Current* (September/October): 35–39.

Sherman, Howard J. 1987. *Foundations of Radical Political Economy.* Part III. Armonk, NY: M.E. Sharpe.

Silverman, Bertram, and Murray Yanowitch. 1997. *New Rich, New Poor, New Russia: Winners and Losers on the Road to Capitalism.* Armonk, NY: M.E. Sharpe.

"Special Issue on the Soviet Union." 1981. *Review of Radical Political Economics* 13, no. 1 (Spring).

Tabb, William K., ed. 1991. *The Future of Socialism: Perspectives from the Left.* New York: Monthly Review Press.

Zimbalist, Andrew, Howard Sherman, and Stuart Brown. 1989. *Comparing Economic Systems: A Political Economic Approach.* Part III. 2d ed. New York: Harcourt Brace Jovanovich.

Eastern Europe

Denitch, Bogdan. 1989. *Limits and Possibilities: The Crisis of Yugoslav Socialism and State Socialist Systems.* Minneapolis: University of Minnesota Press.

Eyal, Gil, Ivan Szelenyi, and Eleanor Townsley. 2001. *Making Capitalism Without Capitalists: The New Ruling Elites in Eastern Europe.* New York: Verso.

Special Issue: "Eastern Europe Goes to Market." 1990. *Dollars & Sense* (July–August).

Zimbalist, Andrew, Howard Sherman and Stuart Brown. 1989. *Comparing Economic Systems: A Political Economic Approach.* Part V. 2d ed. New York: Harcourt Brace Jovanovich.

China

Albert, Michael, and Robin Hahnel. 1981. *Socialism Today and Tomorrow*. Boston: South End Press, ch. 3.

Gabriel, Satya. 2001. *Political Economy of China*. A Smith College course with online readings: www.mtholyoke.edu/courses/sgabriel/chinasmith.html.

Hinton, William. 1990. *The Great Reversal: The Privatization of China, 1978–1989*. New York: Monthly Review Press.

———. 1998. "The Importance of Land Reform in the Reconstruction of China." *Monthly Review* (July/August): 147–160.

Lippit, Victor. 1987. *The Economic Development of China*. Armonk, NY: M.E. Sharpe.

Minqi, Li. 1996. "China: Six Years After Tiananmen." *Monthly Review* (January): 1–13.

Zimbalist, Andrew, Howard Sherman, and Stuart Brown. 1989. *Comparing Economic Systems: A Political Economic Approach*. 2d ed. New York: Harcourt Brace Jovanovich, ch. 11.

Reforming Capitalism: Economic Democracy

Benello, C. George, Len Krimerman, Frank Lindenfeld et al. 1992. *From the Ground Up: Essays on Economic Democracy*. Boston: South End Press.

Bluestone, Barry, and Irving Bluestone. 1992. *Negotiating the Future: A Labor Perspective on American Business*. New York: Basic Books.

Bowles, Samuel et al., 1992. *After the Wasteland: A Democratic Economics for the Year 2000*. Armonk, NY: M.E. Sharpe.

Bowles, Samuel, and Herbert Gintis, eds. 1998. *Recasting Egalitarianism: New Rules for Communities, States, and Markets*. New York: Verso.

Carnoy, Martin, and Derek Shearer. 1980. *Economic Democracy: The Challenge of the 1980s*. Armonk, NY: M.E. Sharpe.

Faux, Jeff, and Gar Alperovitz. 1984. *Rebuilding America*. New York: Pantheon.

Grassroots Economic Organizing Newsletter (GEO): http://geonewsletter.org.

Gunn, Christopher. 1984. *Workers' Self-Management in the United States*. Ithaca, NY: Cornell University Press.

Gunn, Christopher, and Hazel Dayton Gunn. 1991. *Reclaiming Capital: Democratic Initiatives and Community Development*. Ithaca, NY: Cornell University Press.

Harrington, Michael. 1982. "What Socialists Would Do in America—If They Could." In *Beyond the Welfare State*, ed. Irving Howe, 238–260. New York: Schocken Books.

Krimerman, Len, and Frank Lindenfeld, eds. 1992. *When Workers Decide: Workplace Democracy Takes Root in North America*. Philadelphia: New Society.

Schweickart, David. 1996. *Against Capitalism*. Boulder, CO: Westview Press.

Social Movements for Radical Reform

Association of Community Organizations for Reform Now (ACORN): www.acorn.org

Center for Cooperatives: www.cooperatives.ucdavis.edu/index.html

Democratic Socialist of America: www.dsausa.org/dsa.html

International Cooperative Alliance: www.ica.coop/ica/ica/index.html

IGC Internet, A Progressive Web site Connecting People and Progressive Groups: www.igc.org/igc/gateway/index.html

Jobs With Justice: www.jwj.org

Labor Party: www.thelaborparty.org

The New Party: www.newparty.org

The Shared Capitalism Institute: www.sharedcapitalism.org/index.html

United for a Fair Economy: www.stw.org

INDEX

ABOUT THE AUTHOR

Charles Barone is a professor of Economics and American Studies at Dickinson College in Carlisle, Pennsylvania, where he also directs the campus affiliate of the National Coalition Building Institute, an international organization working to eliminate racism and other forms of prejudice and discrimination. He specializes in the political economy of wealth and income distribution, labor issues, and race, class, and gender discrimination.